Office
Wit & Wisdom

Office
Wit & Wisdom

Tracey Turner

PRION

Thanks to the following for opening the kimono:

Tom Battersby, Mike Goldsmith, Karen Ball, Jane Burnard, Marika Thorogood, Sally Trelford, Caroline and Damian Dinning and Alex Webb.

First published in Great Britain in 2004 by

Prion
an imprint of the
Carlton Publishing Group
20 Mortimer Street
London W1T 3JW

10 9 8 7 6 5 4 3 2

Text copyright © Tracey Turner 2004
Design copyright © Carlton Publishing Group 2004

ISBN 1 85375 540 0

A catalogue record for this book is available from the British Library.

Typeset by e-type, Liverpool
Printed in Great Britain by Mackays

CONTENTS

Introduction

If you work in an office now, worked in an office in the past or are intending to work in an office in the future, this book is for you. If you have already experienced office life, you'll know that it's unmitigatedly ghastly. An ability to laugh through the pain is essential if any of us is to survive it.

All sorts of different companies and organizations have offices. But no matter what the organization, all offices share some common horrors:

- A lot of people in a limited amount of space
- Colleagues who might be desperately annoying, unpleasant or insane
- An office hierarchy, which means ... managers
- Office politics
- Office technology with its many pitfalls
- Office parties
- Stress caused by overwork or any of the above

As a typical office worker you might also have to sit through seemingly endless meetings, give stress-inducing presentations

> *Term, holidays, term, holidays, till we leave school, then work, work, work till we die.*
> **C. S. Lewis**

and listen to torrents of mindless management-speak. This book will provide you with a cynical perspective on the corporate nightmare which might help you cope with it. Plus, if you've heard your colleagues talking about paradigm shifts, low-hanging fruit, contributive synergy and arrow-shooters, there is a comprehensive Dictionary of Management-Speak starting on page 139 which could help you to work out what they're on about.

Companies pretend to be caring organizations that have a responsibility towards their employees and want them to live happy and fulfilled lives. In reality it is the aim of every company to take young, healthy individuals, suck them dry of energy, creativity and enthusiasm and then spit out the desiccated husks with never a backward glance.

However, few of us realize this immediately and most enter the world of work assuming that our working lives will be fulfilling, enjoyable and intellectually stimulating. All too often the sad truth reveals itself with brutal swiftness upon our arrival in the office. We realize we are doomed to carry out some thankless and mind-numbing task for a paltry salary, surrounded by colleagues with the social conscience of a Great White, in an atmosphere of deep anxiety caused by the constant threat of redundancy. Welcome to the dark pit of despair that is office life.

Anyone expecting displays of integrity, honesty and decorum is in for a nasty surprise, too. It becomes obvious after the first couple of weeks that office workers lie to cover their own backs, back-stab, brown-nose, self-aggrandize and denigrate others to make themselves look good: the grim world of office politics is revealed. (See the Office Politician's Handbook on page 33 for more on dishonest manoeuvring for personal gain.) It would be unfortunate but not uncommon to arrive in a new office to discover that your boss is a spineless paranoiac who spends all his energy struggling for his own promotion, at least one of your co-workers is barking mad, and your closest colleague harbours a deep-seated hatred towards you because he wanted the job you have.

And yet, despite the various opportunities for humiliation, disappointment and extreme stress inherent in office life, people go to a great deal of trouble to enter it.

The Art of Effective CVs

Many job applicants take on the task of CV compiling with a certain amount of dread. But in fact it can be very satisfying if you see your CV as an opportunity for fun and creativity. The good thing about applying for office jobs is that it's unlikely to make a meaningful difference to anything if you can't actually do what you say you can, which means it's fine to lie through your teeth.

Everyone knows that CVs are very often complete works of fiction – the skill lies in making them sound plausible. You need to make creative use of both management-speak (see the dictionary) and the art of job titlage (to make a really stupid noun out of an ordinary one, which is itself one of the keys to management-speak). What follow are some general tips:

- Some people like to sum themselves up in a perky sentence that goes at the top of their CV. Something along the lines of 'a creative, self-motivated team player with a positive, forward-looking attitude and an impressive skill set'. In an ideal world these people would be bound and gagged and locked in a cupboard. Sadly, many managers find this kind of thing impressive.

- If you are an Office Assistant, it will sound a lot more impressive if you say on your CV that you are an Administrative and Operational Procedures Co-ordinator, or similar. (See the Job Title Fabricator on page 39.) Give yourself free rein in your descriptions of your current job's duties. Have you ever made tea for someone? That's liaising and/or co-operating/communicating with internal departments. Taking minutes counts as devising strategies. And if you can 'project manage' something, even if it's the tea-making rota, that always sounds impressive.

- You might be asked to state your current salary on your CV. There is an unwritten law that says you must exaggerate this as far as possible. The question is, how much can you get away with without arousing suspicion? Here are some guidelines.

> *When a man tells you that he got rich through hard work, ask him: 'Whose?'*
>
> **Don Marquis**

Up to £20,000: add £2,500
Between £20,000 and £30,000: add £3,500
Between £30,000 and £40,000: add £5,000
Over £40,000: pick a number

It goes without saying that, if you think these guidelines are too conservative, trust your instinct and increase the amount. Confidence is the key here: few people will be suspicious unless you look guilty. Of course, if you get the job, the truth will be revealed the minute anyone checks what you've said about salary against your P60. But no one checks.

- Similarly, employers hardly ever check your qualifications. I think you'll find that the number of GCSEs and A Levels you passed has just dramatically increased. If you have a degree, you will now find that it's a First. It's like magic! You might be tempted to stretch this point and say that you have a completely fictitious degree from an establishment you've never even seen. This is fine, as long as you accept that one day you will be caught because you don't

---

 True Office Tales: A Canterbury Tale

The Archbishop of Canterbury sacked his Dean in 2001 when a fictitious PhD on his CV was revealed. So bear that in mind the next time you consider pretending to be a Doctor of Theology to a high-ranking member of the clergy.

> *If you pay peanuts, you get monkeys.*
> **James Goldsmith**

remember the 1996 debagging incident or something similar, and it will be horribly embarrassing.

- Account for periods of unemployment or extended travel creatively – this can be especially useful if you've spent several years as a member of a cult. Make up a job (with a company sadly no longer in business), or perhaps you were 'freelancing'?
- Another alternative is lying about your age. You'll want to get rid of a few years if, for example, you've performed spectacularly badly and are still an assistant dogsbody after five years of hard office toil. Or it could be that you've miraculously achieved office superstardom at a very young age and worry that people won't take you seriously if you reveal your youth. The most common type of age adjustment is downwards, though, usually to avoid being thought of as under-achieving and middle-

---

 True Office Tales: What Not To Put on Your CV

The following have all appeared on real CVs:

- 'I will take the chaos of your office and reform it into a semblance of simple disorder.'
- 'Graduated in the top 66% of my class.'
- 'I am a rabid typist.'
- 'Personal Goal: to hand-build a classic cottage from the ground up using my father-in-law.'
- 'I am very detail-oreinted.'

---

aged. You will need to be on your guard as there will always be the worry that a colleague in a new office could remember you from school or college. Try to have a plausible excuse ready for all eventualities. Or you could, of course, simply leave your age off the CV altogether, forcing the reader to do some maths based on when you got your academic qualifications. Most people aren't very good at maths.

- Offices are dominated by technology so you might find it helps if you exaggerate your familiarity with various different kinds of software. Later, when your total incompetence is revealed, you can always say 'I used a different version' or 'It was a while ago now – amazing how quickly you forget'. People also lie about real technical qualifications, too. Sometimes they get lucky and manage to learn the necessary skills on the job, but often they are found out and publicly shamed.

- If you left your last office under a cloud, don't worry: employers rarely take up references. But if you don't want to put referees on your CV, the line 'references available on request' is useful – the HR department will probably forget about it.

- If you have no office experience at all, you will be deprived of the opportunity to make your current job doing the filing sound as though you are running the company single-handedly from your desk in the corridor. The temptation will be to list some of your more impressive-sounding GCSE results, your swimming certificates and perhaps even include a little section headed 'Good Deeds'. Resist it at all costs. Instead, fabricate some voluntary work which used relevant skills in some way, or discover that you edited your college magazine.

- The commonly included Hobbies and Interests section is a problematic part of CV writing. Naturally, you don't want to reveal that your hobbies are watching reality television and binge-drinking. But who is going to care if your interests include reading, swimming and going to the cinema? A common but entertaining pitfall is to list an array of dangerous sports in a pitiful attempt to seem exciting. Some creative CV writers see this section as an opportunity to show that they are good team players (football, basketball, etc.), are healthily competitive (squash or similar) and can also be motivational leaders (captain of one of the teams). Why not make up something as a talking point (make sure you research it thoroughly), such as keeping iguanas or hang-gliding? Note: if you need a talking point and this isn't your first job, you are in trouble.

People have been adjusting the truth on their CVs since the dawn of office time, but only a tiny proportion of 'adjusters' ever gets found out.

The Interview

You will know your CV has done its work when you are asked to an interview. The prospect of getting out of your current nightmarish office job might make you overly excited

> *It has become an article of the creed of modern morality that all labour is good in itself – a convenient belief to those who live on the labour of others.*
>
> **William Morris**

at this point, but calm yourself with the thought that all offices are dreadful and the next one is more than likely to have its own special brand of unpleasantness.

What to wear to an interview can be problematic. But, assuming that you've arrived at the interview wearing normal clothes as opposed to pyjamas or a sarong and flip-flops, the talking bit is the real minefield.

 True Office Tales: Underqualified

There are thousands of real-life examples of people lying comprehensively on their CVs and in interviews and ending up with office jobs for which they are completely unqualified. (Of course, there are plenty of examples of this in non-office jobs too, but they tend to have far more serious consequences.) Primrose Humprider* got a job as a highly paid executive in a licensing company due largely to a CV which had stretched and embroidered the truth to such an extent that no one would guess her only true qualifications were being upper middle-class, shouting a lot and having a stupid laugh. She made up for her lack of knowledge and experience by being shrewish and unpleasant, barking at everybody as if she knew what she was doing and blaming other people for her mistakes. Although she alienated junior staff and many of her customers, it didn't seem to make any difference to the success of the business, and she was able to stay in the job for seven years, before becoming Managing Director of a large company in a related field, which she knew nothing about either.

* made-up name

> *Nine to five, what a way to make a living;*
> *Barely getting by, it's all taking and no giving.*
> **Dolly Parton, 'Nine to Five'**

Those Tricky Interview Questions and How to Answer Them:

Why do you want this job/to work for this company?

Never tell the truth – that the job offers more money and better holidays for what seems like less work. You're supposed to have thoroughly researched the company and committed the job ad to memory, ready for regurgitation at this point in the interview.

Why are you leaving your current job?

No matter how much you have come to despise your colleagues, depressing working environment and repetitive routine, never mention any of this. You are looking for new opportunities, having achieved your goals in your current position.

What interests you about our product?

This can be particularly difficult if the product is something that bores you rigid. If you really want or need the job you will have to come up with something that sounds convincing. Perhaps a heart-warming story of an incident involving the product at a formative age?

How do you fit into the corporate structure at your current job?

This question gets asked because everyone knows that job titles are meaningless and vary from company to company, and that half of them are made up by the interviewee anyway.

> *Most memorable ... was the discovery (made by all the rich men in England at once) that women and children could work twenty-five hours a day in factories without many of them dying or becoming excessively deformed. This was known as the Industrial Revolution.*
> **W. C. Sellar and R. J. Yeatman, *1066 and All That***

Try to ensure that what you say roughly fits in with whatever job title you've made up.

✉ True Office Tales: What Not To Do in Interviews

The following have all happened in real interviews:

- A candidate telling the interviewer that he didn't want the job he had applied for, but that he had to prove to the Jobcentre that he was actively seeking employment.
- Singing and dancing during an interview as a demonstration of hobbies and interests.
- Offering to have a tattoo of the company logo as proof of loyalty.
- Staging a telephone call supposedly from a rival company with a job offer.

What are your weaknesses?

Sloth, greed, poor time-keeping, inability to meet deadlines, unappealing personal habits ... none of these will sound good. Candour is obviously not an option, but you must also resist the temptation to say that your weaknesses are 'being too much of a perfectionist and working too hard'. The safest response is to pick a small area of training that is peripheral to the job, preferably one that's easy to learn, and state that as your weakness, stressing your willingness to learn in order to rectify this dreadful flaw.

What motivates you?

Rather than being honest and mentioning money, it's best to talk about opportunies to learn and further your career.

How many hours are you prepared to work?

This is a danger sign. Obviously, what the interviewers want to hear is 'As many as it takes to get the job done, even if that means not sleeping and staying in the office all weekend. I am prepared to die from overwork if that's what it takes.' It could mean that, in common with more and more offices, this is an environment where staying late and taking work home is expected and/or seen as a badge of loyalty to the company.

Interview Danger Signs

Don't forget that an interview is also there for you to make your mind up about the company. You might not have been completely honest on your CV, but remember that your interviewers probably won't be absolutely truthful either. You're not likely to be told directly that your boss is a sociopath, twelve-hour days are common, or that you will be sharing a desk with someone so unbearable that the job turnover time is roughly two months. See if you can catch your interviewers out on important areas such as promotion prospects and working conditions. Look out for the danger signs. Do you really want to work in this office?

All paid jobs absorb and degrade the mind.
Aristotle

Danger Signs to Look Out For When Attending an Interview

- mad-eyed employees running down corridors clutching armfuls of paperwork
- shouting/raised voices
- the sound of whooping
- motivational posters displayed in prominent positions
- a colourful 'Suggestions Box' bearing the legend 'We Do Care What You Think'
- sleeping bags under desks or other signs of overnight occupancy
- employees looking dishevelled, grey-faced and red-eyed
- unusually high percentage of ticcing or Touretting among office workers
- people displaying any of the signs of stress on page 64.
- dead plants, worn carpeting – office generally down-at-heel
- a brightly coloured 'creative room' containing beanbags
- high-fiving

Unfortunately, for your first office job you probably won't have much choice but to accept a job that is tedious, regarded with disdain by colleagues and ridiculously underpaid. You might even find that it only exists due to bad management, making it even more depressing.

> *When we talk about equal pay for equal work, women in the workplace are beginning to catch up. If we keep going at this current rate, we will achieve full equality in about 475 years. I don't know about you, but I can't wait that long.*
> **Lya Sorano**

True Office Tales: What's the Point?

Enid's* entry-level clerical job in the early 1990s mainly consisted of checking and correcting any addition or subtraction mistakes in columns of hand-entered figures. At the end of each week, the figures had to be collated and posted – on heavy rolls of paper – to five different outside depots. Needless to say, Enid had lost the will to live by day two. After several months – and despite the fact that her brain had by this time turned into a sort of porridge – Enid noticed that two of the depots' addresses had been wrongly entered, and on checking discovered that one set of figures was being sent to a private address in Rugby and another was mysteriously arriving somewhere that didn't exist. No one had noticed for two years. Happily, this freed up many useful hours for Enid.

Salaries

You might fill in an application form, struggle through two or even three interviews, and complete several different kinds of test, all without knowing what the salary is. It's an unwritten rule that you're not allowed to ask about it until the final interview – by which time you'll have spent many precious hours of your life applying for a job that could well have a salary way below anything you could accept. You might be surprised at the exceptional meanness of some companies, even when they know your current salary from your CV or application form.

* Name changed to protect the innocent

You will notice that most companies offer a *competitive* salary when they advertise for new staff. Obviously, it's not the best salary possible, or they'd say so. It could be the worst and still be 'competing', though.

Psychometric Tests

Psychometric testing is sometimes a part of the interview process. This is in itself a danger sign – be aware that the Human Resources department at this company is at best misguided and at worst insane.

You will be expected to answer a very long list of very boring questions about whether or not you see yourself as a team player, without falling asleep. As a practice exercise, we have devised the following psychometric test. It will uncover whether or not you are suited to working in an office environment, using a selection of subtle psychological methods. Remember, it is impossible to cheat on a psychometric test: just answer honestly and we will be in touch if you've given answers that lead us to believe that you are easily manipulated and prepared to work hard for very little money.

Which of the following statements most applies to you?

1. a) I am generally sociable and outgoing.
   b) I yearn to live as a hermit and grow a long and unhygenic beard.

2. a) I am happiest when part of a team.
   b) I am generally depressed in any social situation, though I am prone to violent mood swings.

3. a) I usually take the initiative if I see an opportunity for improvement.
   b) I seldom do anything unless threatened by someone in authority.

4. a) I am a good problem-solver.
   b) When faced with a problem, I tend to ignore it and hope that it'll go away.

5. a) I am organised and keep careful records.
   b) In my last job I kept iguanas in the filing cabinet.

Read the statements and tick one box:

6. People should always take their quota of sick days: they are just like paid holiday.

   Strongly agree ☐ **Agree** ☐ **Disagree** ☐ **Strongly disagree** ☐

7. Violence can sometimes represent an answer to a workplace dispute.

   Strongly agree ☐ **Agree** ☐ **Disagree** ☐ **Strongly disagree** ☐

8. The internet should be used solely for work purposes, but using it for relaxation, workplace japes, shopping and house-hunting are also permissable.

   Strongly agree ☐ **Agree** ☐ **Disagree** ☐ **Strongly disagree** ☐

9. I can rarely be bothered to assist a colleague who is experiencing difficulty.

Strongly agree ☐ **Agree** ☐ **Disagree** ☐ **Strongly disagree** ☐

10. It's fine to get drunk during your lunch hour if there's a slow afternoon ahead.

Strongly agree ☐ **Agree** ☐ **Disagree** ☐ **Strongly disagree** ☐

Commuter Hell

The journey to and from the office should be given thorough consideration before you sign a contract giving up your right to choose your own hours, make personal phone calls or think personal thoughts between the hours of nine and five. It can become almost as much of a drain on your life-blood and sense of self-worth as the office itself.

Most office workers have to make a journey to work that lasts between 30 and 90 minutes. Some take on a hellish commute of several hours. This journey is made at roughly the same time as everyone else, twice a day. The result of this is sweaty, smelly, cramped and uncomfortable. As if this weren't enough, it's expensive, unreliable and you run the additional risk, over time, of succumbing to commuter rage, which could result in serious physical harm.

Take an average journey to work: a 10-minute walk to the train station, a 20-minute train journey, a 15-minute tube-ride and a five-minute walk to the office. The whole journey should take less than an hour but this doesn't take into account the fact that there are two separate public transport elements. So an average journey adds on fifteen minutes or so because of delays on either the train or the tube. This is frustrating in a low-level kind of way, but once a week or so there's an extra journey time of half an hour because of a more serious problem: something to do with the weather is a popular one. So, once a week you can expect to come home or arrive at the office simmering with rage because your commute has taken 60 per cent longer than it should have done. Every so often, this weekly half-hour delay will make you late for some essential office event, making you boil with uncontrollable fury and possibly attempt to throttle a fellow commuter.

The unreliability of public transport would be enough to cause apoplexy on its own, but commuters have the added problem of other commuters. Being wedged into a small space with unattractive strangers is never much fun, and it's made worse by the ubiquitous Commuters from Hell, including (in ascending order of unpleasantness):

- Backpack wearers
- Broadsheet readers with no newspaper-folding skills
- Headphone wearers – there is no 'acceptable volume'
- Shameless seat stealers
- Bargers
- Noisy chewers

> *Work is the curse of the drinking classes.*
> **Oscar Wilde**

- People who have bathed in a vat of perfume
- People who bray into their mobile phones
- People who bathe very rarely
- Gropers

It's no surprise that commuter rage is on the increase. However, if you manage not to start screaming uncontrollably yourself, witnessing transport rage in others can be reasonably entertaining. Watching a commuter who has decided to make a stand against transgressors of the commuter code has its attractions – well, relative to *not* being distracted from the fact that you're standing with your nose wedged in a stranger's armpit, that is. Most cases of commuter rage in this country live up to the British stereotype and begin with hard stares, continue with some loud coughing and tutting and end with raised voices and everyone taking a very dim view of the situation. Only rarely do they erupt into physical violence. However, there was a recent case of a deranged Oxford–London commuter who threw a rail worker on to the tracks when he missed his train. If you fear you might be teetering on the brink of commuter-related violence, you will be better off visiting one of the many websites exclusively devoted to moaning about particular public transport services. It is the British way.

After several years you will find that the office commute has worn you down to a grey shadow of your former self. It's easy to spot someone who isn't a regular commuter – they are the ones looking surprised or outraged when a cancellation is announced, or when the train remains stuck in a tunnel for several hours. These people are yet to have the spirit drained out of them by thousands of hours of being herded through an overcrowded and underfunded transport system. Everyone else has the blank stare of grim resignation.

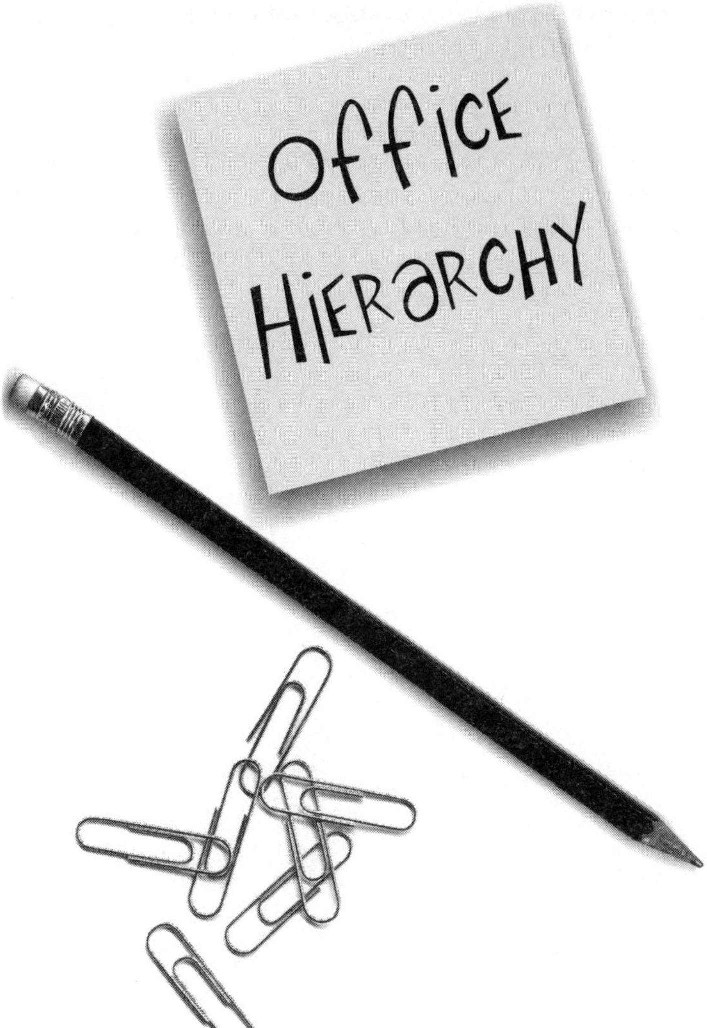
Office
Hierarchy

In most offices, the company hierarchy is explained in the form of a complicated organizational chart designed to look as little as possible like a representation of the feudal system. However, it fools nobody.

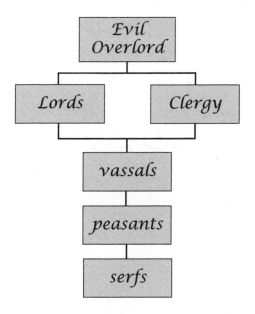

The office hierarchy is one of the most depressing and embittering things about office life because, like the feudal system, it bears no relation to merit whatsoever. The people at the top are the most hard-nosed and/or brown-nosed, skilled in office politics and – often – little else. Some of them aren't skilled in anything at all – their positions of power remain a mystery as well as a deep source of annoyance. The system is reinforced with subtle and not-so-subtle behaviour, conventions and privileges (see page 41). It's the equivalent of living in a troop of baboons and having to present the best bananas to the alpha male. But at least the chief baboon displays strong social and leadership qualities.

The climb up the greasy pole of office hierarchy is so attractive because the lower down you are the more likely you are to be treated like a half-witted personal slave. Generally speaking, about 35 per cent of people in positions of authority are woefully inadequate both professionally and socially but have found that doing something unpleasant to someone who can't do much about it makes them feel marginally better about themselves. These people are likely to wield their power in a variety of unpleasant and upsetting ways (see page 48).

This dysfunctional environment results in a strong desire among employees to scramble up the corporate ladder by whatever means present themselves, with no thought for dignity, fairness, pride or consideration for others. This ruthless and ugly struggle for power is known as …

Office Politics: The Hierarchical Wrestling Match

The skilled office politician uses a variety of Machiavellian manoeuvring with the intention of bringing about his or her own rise to power as swiftly as possible. Office politics can be very obvious – for example, shameless brown-nosing. But the most effective office politician plays a more subtle game whenever possible.

The Office Politician's Handbook

Make sure you are aligned with those in power or those headed for it.

It goes without saying that you should toady to anyone above you in the hierarchy, but there's more to it than that. Be aware of who is likely to be promoted, who is out of favour with the top bosses, who is easily manipulated or timid – make your strategic strikes based on this information. Added to this, ensure that you find out as much office gossip as possible so that you can gauge who is in and out of favour. You might find that a wall chart helps you keep track of things.

Never admit an error.

If you make a mistake that unfortunately falls under the corporate spotlight, there is no choice but to admit that something has gone wrong. However, you will find that it is in no way your fault: there are various circumstances that caused the error. For example, if you are responsible for proof-reading the cover of the company brochure, which then gets printed with a spelling mistake in the title, immediately send an email complaining about ludicrously tight turnaround times and the lack of a dedicated proof-reader in the office, for which you've been campaigning (whether you have or not). Your email should imply that you are in charge of the project without being directly responsible for the error. Never say that anything is your fault, no matter how obvious it is, or how small the mistake.

Cultivate friendships only with colleagues at the same or higher levels.

It's important that you're friendly towards all staff (unless someone is openly trying to thwart you), but don't make the mistake of fraternizing with those of lower rank.

Exaggerate your achievements.

Management-speak is a useful tool here (see page 139). You will find that you spend a lot of time synergizing and enhancing and/or optimizing business development. If you do ever manage to achieve anything exceptional, exploit the opportunity to tell everyone in the company. Send emails to the entire office telling of your triumphs, both real and imagined. Better still, see if you can get someone else to do this for you.

> There is nothing so pleasing to the typical manager as the sound of his own voice echoing through the empty heads of an ignorant workforce.
>
> **John Mitchell**

Campaign for more staff and ensure that you end up managing them.

Complain consistently that you have too much work to do and back this up by working long hours (at least slightly longer than your boss's). Even if you have hardly any work to do, it's amazing how easy it is to convince people that you are overloaded (unless they know exactly what you do on a very detailed level). Explain your reasons for needing to have these people under your management – your boss will probably be quite happy to be persuaded because he or she won't want the extra burden of yet more performance reviews. Once you get your staff, immediately offload any menial tasks, freeing yourself up for further manoeuvring. If your staff don't have enough to do, use your imagination: extra work can be invented easily. It is vital that the office politician is never seen doing anything menial.

Claim good ideas as your own and appropriate other people's original thoughts.

If you hear someone voice an impressive idea or opinion, or just a good 'sound-bite', simply start using it yourself. No one will know you didn't think of it yourself, apart from the person whose idea it is, so make sure they're not in a position to thwart you – preferably it should be someone who reports to you. It's very difficult for someone to say, 'Hey, that was *my* idea!' You can bank on the fact that they won't.

Demand a job title that's different from your peers'.

This is important but might be difficult to justify. If you have successfully managed to attain a higher level of staff reporting to you than colleagues doing the same job, this is a huge help. Words like 'Senior', 'Managing' and 'Leader' are useful. Be creative. (See the Job Title Fabricator on page 39.)

Never openly criticize company policy.

Depending on the company you work for, you may have to swallow a lot of corporate nonsense (although it is possible for the skilled office politician to convince himself that it all makes perfect sense). However ludicrous the policy, think of something positive to say about it in case you're asked.

Subtly imply greater power or influence than you have.

For example, send an email praising a colleague on the same level as you: many people will infer from this that you manage your colleague. Those who don't will at least see your gesture as generous, and your colleague can hardly complain, even if he or she realizes the true purpose of your machinations. Of course, make sure that your praise isn't given for something all that impressive.

Claim successful projects.

Make sure you become involved in any office project or department that is causing a stir. Talk about them often to promote the perception that whatever it is couldn't have happened without you.

Never make your back-stabbing obvious.

Of course, back-stabbing is essential for the office politician, but nobody will admit openly to approving of it, so you must make sure it's heavily disguised. Raised eyebrows during a meeting, as if surprised and concerned to hear the views of your colleague, can be effective.

Be vocal and enthusiastic in meetings.

What you say is less important than being noticed. If you can't think of anything blindingly original to say (which will almost certainly be the case), voice your approval of a strategically chosen superior's views.

Try not to laugh in triumph in the manner of an evil villain ('Nyar har har har!').

This will give the game away and undo all of your hard work.

Much of the office politician's success depends on how much they can subtly imply without sounding nasty, and how successfully they can manipulate their colleagues. Typically, office politicians have no real talent for the job they're supposed to be doing, which is the reason they put so much time and energy into reaching senior management as quickly as possible.

Job Titles

Job titles are an obvious signifier of an employee's standing within the company (although not always – see page 40). Until you are the CEO or equivalent, there's always a better job title out there, beckoning coyly.

Some companies have extremely rigid rules about job titles and you won't be able to influence your own – other than on your CV, naturally. But in many offices, the way is open for creative suggestions about your title.

Use the Job Title Fabricator opposite to give yourself a title more befitting your expertise, wisdom and flair. For example, if you manage the office supplies, perhaps you should be called a Senior Functionality Manager. You could have almost any office job – even one that is totally unnecessary – and put 'Business Development' into your title, perhaps accompanied by 'Specialist', 'Facilitator', 'Leader' or 'Analyst'. Simply pick an appropriate word from either two, or three if you think you can get away with it,* of the lists opposite to fabricate an impressive-sounding job title.

It goes without saying that you should only choose words such as 'Associate' if it's the only way you can use an otherwise very grand title – everyone knows it really means 'Assistant'. And of course avoid 'Assistant' completely – if this is part of your current job title, set to work immediately to remove it. Be aware that job titles can mean very different

---

* If you feel you are able to choose words from all three lists, you probably work in an environment of sheer corporate lunacy. This is also true if you feel able to include the word 'Architect' (unless you design buildings) or 'Orchestrator'.

Job Title Fabricator

1	2	3
Business	Functionality	Orchestrator
Technical	Optimization	Specialist
Senior	Configuration	Developer
Managing	Interactive	Architect
Market	Quality	Facilitator
Brand	Expansion	Technician
Value	Development	Co-ordinator
Project	Management	Analyst
Principal	Product	Leader
Associate	Creative	Manager
Executive	Growth	Officer
Developmental	Excellence	Consultant
Strategic	Product	Director

things in different companies. For example, 'Executive' can be another euphemism for 'Assistant' in some offices, while in others it might mean a corner office and a company car; sometimes 'Leader' is seen to be a better title than 'Manager'. Make sure you know the context in your office.

Because the meaning of job titles varies so wildly from company to company, it's difficult to make any sense of them at all from outside the specific environment. You might be an Office Manager in one company, move to another doing exactly the same job and find yourself a Strategic

Development Co-ordinator. But in office life, true meaning is far less important than the hierarchical struggle.

Job titles aren't always invented by the person doing the job, of course. A new job title is often a response by a manager to an employee's request for recognition and reward. Or sometimes it's a money-saving exercise: one office worker was mystified as to why her colleague was promoted above her until she discovered that her new boss was earning £8,000 per year less than her even after the promotion. Giving someone a posh job title is a lot easier, and makes more financial sense, than paying them more money. Titles such as 'Executive', 'Senior' or 'Principal' are often given without an accompanying pay rise. If you're described as a manager but don't actually manage anyone, you can be sure that your job title exists either to make you feel big and important without the necessity of paying you extra money, or to make someone else feel bad.

Your True Place in the Hierarchy

You can't always rely on your job title to tell you your place in the office hierarchy. It's not out of the question to find yourself in an office where every position has an insanely convoluted title, making it impossible to tell from the outside who reports to whom, who does the photocopying, who gets to go on luxurious all-expenses-paid business trips, and who gets the bananas.

There are, however, other ways to assess status when you're on the inside of an office. Every office worker is keenly tuned to the little things that reveal the pecking order. These hierarchical benchmarks seem insignificant, and they're not often mentioned, yet people would fight to the death over them.

To determine your true place in the hierarchy, ask yourself the following questions:

How often do you make the tea?
Few office workers, whatever their status, expect to have tea and coffee made for them by an underling. Nevertheless, the higher up you are the less tea-making you will perform.

Are people nice to you? How nice?
You would be foolish to suppose that people in offices are being nice to you out of pure goodwill. Most office workers only bother being pleasant to colleagues if they fear there might be repercussions otherwise. If you've ever been a temporary worker in an office you will have had this forcefully demonstrated by the fact that no one even speaks to you unless absolutely necessary, going so far as to have conversations across you as if you weren't there.

How many email groups are you part of?
If the only email group you're in is your departmental one, you're just making up the head count. Higher up the hierarchy, you might find yourself in a department group, a management group (the more of these the higher your

status) and specific task force groups (again, several of these: you will be in a consultancy role). The number of 'FYI' emails you receive is also a mark of your position in the company.

How many meetings do you attend?

Some companies have a meeting every time a member of staff sneezes, so this status measure is relative. You can judge for yourself which are the important ones that signify where you are on the corporate ladder.

How up to date is your technology?

IT departments don't hand out the latest gear to the people who need it most (often they're the last to receive it) but to those of the highest rank. If you're always one of the first people to be given better computer equipment, particularly if it looks flashy, you're near the top of the company heap.

Do you have a company car?

In most companies, once people reach a certain level they are offered a company car whether or not they need one for their job. If you have a company car, it's necessary to talk about it as often as possible because otherwise your colleagues may not know you have one – after all, you can't park it by your desk. It's not too difficult to bring your car into the conversation: offer to give people lifts in it to attend outside meetings. Explain that it's no problem: you can use your *company car*.

Do you go on business trips?

Of course, this depends on the industry you're in: you might go on lots of business trips and still be struggling for air in an overcrowded office the rest of the time. But there is often fierce competion over who gets to go to trade fairs in exotic locations, for example. These desirable trips are a good indicator of seniority.

How often do you talk to the person in the highest position in the company?

If you find it necessary to talk to the CEO every day, and you are not his or her assistant or chauffeur, you are probably fairly high up the corporate ladder.

Do you have an assistant?

In some companies, an assistant is bestowed upon you only when you reach the very highest levels of the organization. Whether or not this is true of your company, having an assistant is still an important mark of your ranking. Obviously, you should refer to your assistant as often as possible, even if you have to share him or her with several other colleagues. (Sharing an assistant can lead to complications – see page 55.)

Do you have your own office?

This is the ultimate acolade. It's a very obvious indicator of status – you can't help but notice if someone is sitting on their own at a desk in a room with real walls, a door and a window rather than being outside with everyone else fighting for space and higher partitions. But even once you've won the coveted prize of your own office, you will no doubt find that within your company there are *better offices than yours*. The most obvious measure of personal office quality is size, but it's by no means the only one. You need to look for further status indicators such as: size and number of windows; amount and quality of office furniture (in some companies, only the higher echelons are given the luxury of chairs with armrests, for example); how many people you can fit around your meeting table – *if you have one*; whether you have controllable air-conditioning; etc.

If you do have your own office, even if it's a windowless dungeon the size of a broom cupboard with a view of the toilets, think yourself very lucky indeed that you're not out there with the common herd. (See page 79 for more on the hell that is open-plan office life.) But there are ways to artificially up your status, even in the open-plan environment (bear in mind that it might be more difficult if you work in a cubicle):

1. Campaign for a desk in a corner of the office with a window.
2. Try arranging your furniture so that it looks as though your area of the office has been cordoned off. Use props such as large plants and notice-boards so that it's difficult for people to see in from the outside. If you share space with a colleague, try to erect some kind of fence between you. This is very nearly a real office.

3. In time, it might even be possible to persuade your boss to erect walls and a door around your area – and an office of your own will be in your grasp. Perhaps you could argue for your walls and door to be part of a package that includes your new fabricated job title.

If you have a corner office of 20 square metres or more with mullioned windows, air-conditioning, large meeting table, several computers all equipped with the latest technology, intercom connected to your team of assistants, a drinks cabinet, a large video projector, and a company private jet awaiting you on the roof, you might think you've reached the top. But there are still higher levels to achieve. Ask yourself questions such as, 'If it suited my fell purposes, how many people could I cause to writhe like worms?' Have you considered going into politics?

Salaries and Bonuses

Salary is the one true indicator of your position in the hierarchy. In the private sector, salaries are often closely guarded secrets for this very reason. This is, of course, a nonsense that should be exploded and yet the situation persists. People are worried that letting their colleagues know how much they are paid will result in either a) taking the blame for any rioting that might ensue; b) humiliation when their true place in the hierarchy is revealed; or c) a pay cut to put their salary in line with those of colleagues on the same level.

Bonuses can vary from several hundred thousand pounds to a luncheon voucher and are another good benchmark of how highly you are valued. If you receive an envelope containing a £10 book token while your colleague opens his and looks enormously smug, you can probably not expect promotion in the near future – to look on the bright side. Some companies do not seem to realize that nothing whatsoever would be an awful lot better than a luncheon voucher and persist with an ungenerous Christmas gift to all their staff, thus upping the bile factor immeasurably.

The Boss

Unless you are Bill Gates you are likely to have some kind of boss. Throughout your office career you will encounter many of them – the good, the bad and the ugly. The majority are mediocre, only occasionally making you want to tear them limb from limb. All you can hope for, unless you get lucky and find a good boss, is that generally your boss will leave you alone enough to allow you to get on with your job.

To be a really good boss, you need the following qualities:

Intelligence
Extensive experience of the job(s) you manage
Integrity
Fairness
Excellent judgement
Enthusiasm for the job

Ability to communicate clearly and effectively
Ability to nurture and encourage your staff
Genuine interest in progressing the careers and job satisfaction of your staff

It's small wonder, then, that most bosses fail miserably. Bosses are at least 80 per cent more likely to display the following than the list of ideals above:

Bitterness, both personal and professional
Neuroses of various types
Paranoia
Unscrupulousness
Lack of enthusiasm
Lack of knowledge
Poor judgement
Unfairness
Fear of talented staff
Nepotism
Utter stupidity

See below for the many and various ways these unappealing traits can be used by terrible bosses to make life hell for anyone unfortunate enough to have to work for them.

Long and learned books have been written on the subject of management styles. In fact, it can all be summed up in two simple equations:

micro-management = interfering too much
macro-management = delegating everything but taking
all the credit

> Smithers, for attempting to kill me, I'm giving you a five per cent pay cut.
> **Mr Burns,** *The Simpsons*

You might find yourself working in an office in which there is a 'flat management structure'. Supposedly, this means that everyone is on more or less the same level, working together as a team. There is a team leader, of course (and probably several levels underneath that exist but aren't acknowledged). In reality, it just means that the boss (sorry, team leader) will dress in casual clothes and think he's groovy, and his staff simply find more subtle ways of brown-nosing to further their careers.

How To Be a Really Terrible Boss

If you manage staff, congratulations. You will find that there are many and various ways to make life hell for them. All of the points below are well documented and no doubt many will already be familiar to you. Choose the methods that best suit your twisted personality.

1. **Never be satisfied with the performance of the people you manage.**
   There's nearly always some little thing to criticize. No matter how well a job has been done, seize upon a small defect and blow it out of all proportion rather than praising your staff for anything.

2. **Take credit for the hard work or ideas of your staff.**
   Present any evidence of work as your own to anyone above you in the hierarchy, whether you've had anything to do with it or not. If a member of your staff comes to

you with an idea, nod wisely and say that you'll deal with it. Write it up as pompously as possible, including a few minor changes and additions, and present it as your own work.

3. **Give free rein to your emotions every so often.**
   Do this by screaming loudly, storming out of the office, throwing things, etc. This is exercising your management right to behave badly. Being shouted at is, of course, utterly humiliating, which is another plus. Everyone else must behave with due decorum at all times: if they don't, punishment should be swift and severe.

 True Office Tales: Sitting Bull

One particular Managing Director went on the warpath so often that he became known as Sitting Bull. His unpredictable mood swings, fits of temper, sudden changes of opinion and tendency to scream at people meant that staff were routinely reduced to tears. During one particularly unpleasant tantrum, for example, he ostentatiously ripped up a report, called the Head of IT a 'shambling moron' and sacked his secretary. When he interviewed prospective employees, one of his questions was whether the interviewee was prone to tears, explaining with surprising candour that he often seemed to make people weep.

4. **Be inconsistent.**

Try lulling your staff into a false sense of security by being extra nice one day and appallingly unpleasant the next. This will make your staff jumpy and add extra stress. You are management and therefore allowed to have moods (see number 3).

5. **Know no inhibition.**

You are really important. Other people will have to understand that if you want to walk around barefoot, in pyjamas, scratching yourself or burping, that must mean it's important to you. You need to feel at home in the office, otherwise your immense wisdom and creativity could be hampered. Your staff should appear smart and professional at all times but, then, they don't have the same pressures on them as you do.

6. **Force staff to work long hours.**

Given that your staff are probably slacking for at least two hours out of the working day, it's only fair that they should be forced to come in early, stay late and perhaps work weekends too. Subtly imply that long hours are the rule rather than the exception and are expected if staff are to keep their jobs. To help engender this atmosphere, sit on projects until they become urgent and only then hand them to your staff; give people complicated tasks just before the end of the working day and say that you need them for nine-thirty the next morning.

7. **Choose a favourite (or favourites) from among your staff.**

   This will help to foster an atmosphere of unhealthy competition among employees. Make sure your choice has nothing whatsoever to do with merit. Once you've picked the lucky member(s) of staff, there's no need for subtlety. Give them plenty of unearned perks, bonuses and promotions. Your other staff will be eaten up with fury at the injustice of it, yet feel powerless to complain.

8. **Say you have an 'open door policy' but growl menacingly when people drop in.**

   This could form part of your inconsistency policy.

9. **Send your staff on personal errands.**

   There's nothing like it for making them feel under-valued and humiliated.

10. **Imply that sick leave is not tolerated.**

    You are forced by law to allow sick leave, but make it clear that the company sees it as a sign of weakness – taking it could affect promotion prospects and pay increases. If you are asked for compassionate leave due to bereavement or similar, again imply that it's not really warranted and shows lack of commitment.

11. **Issue impossible demands.**

    Such as, 'Sort out my unfeasibly disorganised office, diary, pile of work that's been sitting there for several months that I've done nothing about, by the time I get back from my long weekend break.' When your staff don't manage to do what you've asked, get angry and reprimand them.

12. **Withold holidays.**
Staff will think they can get away with anything if you just grant them holiday any time they ask for it. When someone asks you for time off, no matter how far in advance, immediately pull a concerned and/or mildly annoyed face. Take a day or so before you issue your formal response. If you do decide to grant the leave, try and make some provisos, such as 'as long as project X is complete before you go'.

13. **Don't do any real work.**
Of course, this is the aim of all bosses – to get the underlings running around doing all the hard graft while you 'take a helicopter view'. The most annoying bosses are those who make no attempt to cover up the fact that all they do is come in late, go for a long lunch, take a little nap and then go home again – though to do this confidently your staff will have to be too afraid of you to blow the whistle. Double your efforts to ensure this is the case.

14. **Chip away at the self-confidence of your staff.**
There are many ways of doing this. Shouting, finding fault and personal errands have already been mentioned, but also remember that personal criticism is often even more effective.

15. **Be suspicious of your staff at all times.**

   Your employees will undoubtedly be idle slackers who will do anything to get out of work and undermine your authority. Check up on them constantly.

 True Office Tales: Suspicious Minds

An extreme example of this type of boss was William Shockley, who started a silicon-chip company in California in the 1950s. He was paranoid about his staff and constantly monitored them, often falsely accusing them of various misdemeanours. He even forced his employees to take a lie-detector test to discover who had caused a minor accident. Not surprisingly, most of the people who worked for Shockley left and started their own companies. In fact so many staff left that, inadvertantly, Shockley had begun the huge expansion of the industry that resulted in Silicon Valley. This, of course, is not the effect you are trying to achieve – it's much better if your staff simply end up miserable and demotivated.

---

16. **Ostentatiously take note of latecomers.**

   Unless, of course, you like to make a point of arriving late at the office yourself. But if you do have a particular horror of lateness, you might want to force any staff who arrive after nine a.m. to sign a late book – hopefully this will remind them of school and add to their feelings of having no control over their lives. It's surprising how many bosses pursue this course of action, some of them going to the extreme of standing guard in reception at nine o'clock.

17. **Be spineless.**
    Never bother fighting for better pay or conditions for the people you manage. Be aggressive and ruthless with those beneath you in the hierarchy, but a grovelling toady to anyone above you.

18. **Blame staff for your own mistakes.**
    It's easy to do this without the knowledge of your staff. You might like to select one scapegoat in particular, although he or she may start to wonder why they are consistently passed over for promotion.

Any one of the above methods, sustained over a period of months, is enough to leave staff unhappy and sapped of energy and enthusiasm. To be a *really* terrible boss, you need to practise at least three of the above on a regular basis. To ensure that your staff absolutely loathe you, make sure that one of them is number three.

Having a Really Terrible Boss

Having a bad boss is just about the worst thing that can happen to you in an office (barring freak accidents and groping incidents). All the usual rules of social behaviour are removed: if this were a different context, you might spend five minutes with your moronic, paranoid, power-crazed manager before getting away as fast as possible and making a mental note never to go anywhere near him ever again, perhaps throwing in a couple of appropriate insults as a parting gesture. But here in the office, you're stuck with him.

The chances are that you won't make it through your working life without encountering a manager you'd like to see roasting on a spit. Imagining him in his death throes is one way of dealing with the situation. Confronting your boss is another – but bear in mind that this can only be effective with a boss who ranks fairly low down on the Insanity-ometer. If he or she is barking mad (as is all too often the case), then your reasonable, calm, intelligent attempts to achieve a better working relationship will result only in a maniacal tirade and your P45.

Personal Assistants

If you are, or ever have been, someone's assistant or secretary, you will know that the Bad Boss problem becomes magnified by about five million when your job exists solely to support your boss's job. Having an assistant – itself a status symbol – brings out the absolute worst in the very worst bosses. They often come to see their assistant as a personal slave, not just performing a job but existing solely

Any new project goes through the following stages: enthusiasm; complication; disillusionment; search for the guilty; punishment of the innocent; decoration of those who did nothing.

Anonymous

True Office Tales: The Paper Trail

Actors' agents are not famous for their modesty, compassion and timidity. Many of them are ruthless, power-crazed sadists who really shouldn't be allowed to have control over any sentient being – and yet all of them have assistants over whom they wield executive power. The assistants, hungry for the day when they can become agents themselves, will put up with almost anything, including (in one US agency) a boss who had a habit of chewing paper and then spitting it out in rank, wet globules all around his office. (See point number five above.) One of his assistant's many duties – and possibly the most humiliating, although it's debatable – was cleaning up the spat paper pulp.

---

to minister to their needs. A Personal Assistant is guaranteed to further inflate any already overblown ego.

The unfortunate assistant's position is made even worse when he or she reports to more than one boss. It is not uncommon for a tug-of-war to develop, each boss trying to outdo the other by making more and more demands on the assistant's time, energy and, ultimately, life-blood.

Performance Appraisals

The purpose of the Performance Appraisal is to perpetrate the myth that the company cares about your level of professional fulfilment and development. Because of this it is, of course, an empty charade. Someone once said that Performance Appraisals can be defined as 'feedback from people who don't want to give it given to people who don't want to receive it', and how right they were.

Most bosses will do all they can to ensure that the very minimum amount of their own time and effort is put into reviewing their staff's performance. Really, they would rather not have to do them at all. This is for a variety of reasons:

1. It's extra work.
2. Fear of demands for more money.
3. Fear of demands for promotion.
4. Fear of criticism ('This is a two-way street!').
5. Potential for embarrassment/humiliation (see above).
6. It's a waste of time.
7. Complicated forms have to be filled in and filed.
8. Describing good performance but making it sound like average performance is quite difficult.
9. It's a bit like an interview, but with someone you know it's even more uncomfortable.
10. Lack of any interest in staff's professional development or opinions.

You've probably noticed how much of the language used in Performance Appraisals is almost completely devoid of meaning. This is because of a conscious effort on the part of managers to make the procedure less uncomfortable by using euphemistic phrases instead of blunt criticism and/or saying more or less the same vague things about all staff to ensure as little time is wasted on them as possible. Help is at hand for the lazy manager who couldn't care less about the staff and can't be bothered to come up with a written appraisal on his or her own: hundreds of books and websites provide stock phrases and answers common in performance reviews (such as 'salary increases are simply not feasible at this time'). So when your manager tells you that you should 'set achievable goals for continuous improvement', be grateful that she's put a lot of time and effort into her appraisal.

Another common ruse is for bosses to try to make their staff do all the work by 'getting their input', which translates as writing the appraisal report for them – the boss will fiddle minimally with whatever you've written and then sign it. This is your chance to say astoundingly brilliant things about yourself, dressed up in a bit of management-speak. It can be fun – particularly if you find your job mind-numbingly dull.

The only really good thing about Performance Appraisals is that they provide you with a golden opportunity to bag as many training courses as possible. You should present training as the answer to all of your problems – including the ones you've made up. See page 102 for the reasons why extra training is such an important goal.

The other main aspect of the Performance Appraisal is

the struggle for more money. It's your job to present yourself as a model worker whose talent knows no bounds (if your boss has asked you to write your own appraisal, this will be easy) and who deserves at least double your current salary. It's your boss's job to mutter about budgets and regretfully decline a salary increase (perhaps with the offer of a ludicrous job title to make up for it), or to grant one of microscopic proportions and attempt to make you feel massively grateful.

We have already considered some of the nightmares inherent in getting an office job and finding a place in the hierarchy. But there are many more aspects of corporate life which make offices hell on earth. Perhaps the most obvious is other staff. The many and various – and mostly dreadful – different types of people commonly found lurking in offices have a whole chapter to themselves, starting on page 121. But as well as your colleagues, the office environment harbours all sorts of other causes of misery and distress.

Stress

Some people find ways of getting around it, but almost everyone who is employed in an office moans about stress, whether they actually do any work or not. Commuting, of course, can be extremely stressful (see page 25), so that many workers have had as much as they can take even before they arrive at the office. Once people do arrive, after several hours stuck in train tunnels or traffic, companies try to wring as much hard toil from them as is possible within

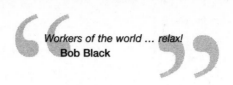

Workers of the world ... relax!
Bob Black

the constraints of law, which is of course another major source of office stress. Added to this, there are managers (see page 46). And then there's the fear of losing your job – however appalling your office is, it seems preferable to living on 50 pence a day.

Some common causes of office stress:

- Sharing office/desk with someone/several people you despise
- Commuting
- Heavy workload
- Insane or unpleasant manager
- Lack of support
- Long hours
- Being unsuited to the job (for example, working in marketing and having a conscience)
- Fear of redundancy

Some common signs of stress:

- Hostile behaviour
- Listlessness/apathy
- Uncontrollable weeping or screaming
- Enraged countenance
- Barking like a dog
- Hand-wringing

> *The time to relax is when you don't have time for it.*
> **Jim Goodwin**

- Pulling out hair
- Asleep at desk

One of the most common causes of office stress stems from the belief that the success of a particular project is vitally important. In the vast majority of office jobs, this is

---

 True Office Tales: The Trouser Render

Some jobs are more stressful than others – in offices stress levels tend to be in direct proportion to the amount of money involved. And of course some people deal with stressful situations a lot better than others – and some deal with it in very strange ways. One US literary agent, who tended to make his emotions known rather forcefully, found himself involved in the most lucrative deal of his career. The shouting and loud crashing noises that could be heard coming from his office over the course of several weeks were a tip-off to other staff that he was under a certain amount of stress. One side of the final conversation between agent and publishing house was conducted at such volume that all the agent's colleagues heard every word, even though it took place behind a closed door. When the agent put down the phone, having made the deal, his colleagues were expecting some kind of grand finale. The agent burst from his office with his hands in his pockets uttering an incoherent growling noise, which increased in volume as he ripped off both his trouser pockets with the force of his pent-up aggression.

---

completely untrue. It's not a matter of life and death, it's a matter of making large sums of money for someone else. Try to bear that in mind the next time you feel the pressure is on.

The stress of a demanding job might lead you to yearn for a job you can totally forget about at the end of the working day. But jobs of this kind tend to have their own stress factors:

- If your job means you're at the bottom of the office hierarchy, unpleasant colleagues will try to assert their superiority over you even if they're not your boss. Colleagues can be a source of stress for a wide variety of reasons – this will always be a risk.
- You will probably have several bosses, multiplying the chances of having a Bad Boss.
- Your job may be mind-numbingly dull, which can be stressful too.
- Realizing that in the eyes of your company you rank somewhere between the coffee machine and the photocopier is not good for anyone's self-esteem.

The Hell of Presentations

Many office employees have to make presentations as part of their job and, for 80 per cent of them, this is a source of deep anxiety and distress. Company policy dictates the number of presentations you are likely to have to give, and of course some organizations and industries are more fond of them than others. Some companies are so wildly keen on presentations that they ask staff to present an hour-long report full of complicated graphs to a packed meeting room on almost any pretext – changes to the menu in the canteen, staff reactions to the new company logo, etc. Office workers with time on their hands and an inflated sense of their own importance might volunteer to give presentations on the slightest pretext, too.

If you have to give presentations and you hate doing it, it's a good idea to campaign for more training. Of all training courses, the ones entitled 'How To Present Effectively' are the least enjoyable because they usually mean that you have to make at least one presentation. However, the fear of horribly embarrassing yourself in front of a large group of people reduces in direct proportion to the number of presentations you have made. It's a good idea to embarrass yourself in front of people who don't have power over your income and general well-being, and there's an added bonus in that you get the chance to laugh at everyone else on the training course embarrassing themselves too.

Working out how to use the presentation software is the fun part. But once you've made your bullet points into a variety of animated zoo animals revolving 360 degrees and entering each slide from a different direction, and you have spent many happy hours contemplating and adjusting your background colours and typefaces, the real problems start when you realize you don't have anything to say.

Fortunately, this doesn't matter. You can put together a convincing presentation on almost any subject – not knowing anything about it can sometimes be a help rather than a hindrance. Simply follow the rules below and your presentation will be a success.

1. **Assess your audience.**
   Are these people likely to be interested in what you have to say? If people are forced to come to your presentation – either explicitly or implicitly – the answer might well be no. If they're from the IT or any other technical department and you're not, the answer is almost certainly no. In addition to the techies and the people who are forced to attend, some people are likely to attend colleagues' presentations voluntarily because they feel like having a little rest, and not because they're interested in the subject. In all likelihood, most of your audience will consist of people whose main objective is to stare into space and drool gently.

   A word of caution, though: beware of people from the finance department because the only thing they will be interested in is your complicated spreadsheets, and they will be unafraid of piping up to point out the various failings and inconsistencies in what you've done – try to ensure they're not invited.

   Once you've assessed your audience you can judge how much time, effort and real information you need to put into your presentation.

2. **Think of five points to make about your subject.**

   Your points don't need to be anything original – in fact, the more blindingly obvious the better. The received wisdom is that your audience will remember no more than five main points, so there's no reason to clutter their minds with more. Think about it: you could come up with five things to say about anything if you had to. As a practice exercise, see if you can think of five things to say about pig-keeping (remember, it doesn't matter how obvious they are). Easy, isn't it?

3. **Include plenty of repetition.**

   Another piece of Presentation Lore is that you should 'Tell them what you're going to tell them, tell them, then tell them what you've told them'. So most of what you say will be repetition anyway – and the good news is that if people are paying attention and notice this, it will be seen as a good thing! Think up lots of different ways of saying exactly the same thing.

4. **Include plenty of statistics.**

   It's an old joke that 75 per cent of statistics are made up, but one that is 98 per cent true. It's very difficult to check most statistics, but if challenged you can say that you got the information from a website that seemed authoritative.

5. **Include spreadsheets.**

   The more complicated the better. This is an opportunity for your audience to glaze over, which will be a good thing if you don't really know what you're talking about. But beware of the finance department, as mentioned above.

6. **Distribute hand-outs either before the meeting or afterwards, depending on whether or not you want your audience to listen to you.**

   This is point number six, so you will probably forget this one instantly. But anyway: if you have hand-outs to give out and you want people to pay attention, don't let your audience have them until your presentation is over. But if you want people to be as distracted as possible from the nonsense you're spouting, distribute hand-outs right at the beginning. If possible, include other things that might prove more interesting than what you're saying – sample products or sweets, perhaps.

Most of what you say will be blindingly obvious, 20 per cent completely made up, and most of the people you're presenting to won't be listening to a word you say. What were you worrying about? You can gauge the success of your presentation easily. Check for obvious signs of a distracted audience (as mentioned above, not necessarily a bad thing):

- Drooling
- Fixed stare, or gazing out of window
- Reading magazine or newspaper
- Yawning

- Notes being passed around, especially if accompanied by sniggering
- Sleeping

Meetings from Hell

In every company there is at least one person whose unofficial job title is Convener of Utterly Pointless Meetings. There might be meetings on how we all feel about the message the company is communicating to its customers, meetings in which everyone gives a little talk about what they're doing at the moment (which in many cases will be panicking due to overwork), meetings to 'touch base' with other departments. It seems that these people must be on some kind of bonus scheme related to the amount of colleagues' time wasted.

Getting out of going to meetings is usually relatively easy, but often your presence at a meeting has more to do with office politics than with any genuine need to be there. If you don't attend the 'interdepartmental liaison' meetings and the rest, you could be seen as *not being a team player* (gasp). (In offices, 'not being a team player' ranks somewhere between 'embezzlement' and 'crapping on the boss's desk' on the scale of corporate crimes.) Or you might find that the person chairing the meeting has a particularly fragile ego accompanied by a pathological desire to avenge real and imagined slights, such as non-attendance at meetings.

So the chances are that you will have to attend many

meetings in which you have no interest whatsoever. Some of them you will probably find intensely irritating. However, the good news is that meetings offer an opportunity to have a little break. If you are forced to go to a long meeting you know you will find annoying, partly because you are extremely busy and will have to work like a caffeine-fuelled chipmunk to make up the time wasted, try not to let it become a source of stress. Instead, use it to have a pleasant rest. Switch off, relax and imagine yourself in a beautiful shady garden listening to the sound of birdsong instead of the nonsense being gibbered by a middle manager in a shiny suit.

Of course, the nightmare scenario is that you are roused from your trance-like state by the sound of your name, followed by, 'What's your view on this?' Perhaps the best idea is to think up some all-purpose, general comment before the meeting for emergencies such as this. But if you've failed to do that, the chances are you will have taken in some of the content of the meeting by osmosis and can think up some kind of response – even if you have to fall back on asking the questioner to elaborate. It will take practice, but you can train yourself to enter a trance-like state reserved for meetings from which you can emerge, bright and alert, on hearing key words.

Bodging budgets

Not many people are good at maths (see quote opposite). The ones who are tend to become accountants, actuaries, bookkeepers or financial advisers. (In fact, financial advisers don't need to be good at maths, they just need to be good at identifying gullible people.)

That leaves the rest of us to grapple hopelessly with budgets and spreadsheets – yet another cause of office stress and anxiety. Why this sort of thing should be part of your job when you've been employed as a graphic designer is anybody's guess.

There are two methods for dealing with budgets: a) copy the last one; and b) make wild and unsubstantiated guesses. Either course of action gives an equal chance of your budget being accurate.

Sick Office Syndrome

Some office environments are healthier than others. But it is fair to say that all of them are seething incubators of a wide variety of bacteria and toxic fumes and represent a serious health hazard. Noxious germs breed in the air-conditioning system, windows are seldom openable, and viral diseases are rife.

Germs are spread by touch or in the air. Fluid from a sneeze can travel three and a half metres, and sneeze droplets can remain suspended in the air for up to twenty minutes. The lack of ventilation common in offices means that you're likely to be breathing in other people's snot every minute of your day in the office. Any shared office equipment, such as the photocopier, computer keyboards

> *All sedentary workers ... suffer from the itch, are a bad color, and in poor condition ... For when the body is not kept moving the blood becomes tainted, its waste matter lodges in the skin, and the condition of the whole body deteriorates.*
> **Bernardino Ramazzini**

and phones, is a morass of infectious bacteria spread by touch.

If everyone in the office was perfectly healthy, these frankly revolting conditions wouldn't matter so much. But of course they're not. People often stagger into the office barely alive due to increasing pressure from managers not to take sick leave. Tell your manager you're feeling ill and he or she will probably recommend a remedy rather than advise you to go home. Have you noticed the recent spate of cold and flu remedy TV ads which imply that if you have a day off you will be doomed to abject failure in your career? The direct result of this is that people come into work when they're ill and spread contagion throughout the office, which ends up like a doctor's waiting-room. We are all doomed to a continuous stream of unpleasant ailments and diseases for the rest of our working lives.

If you are still in any doubt at all about the unhealthiness of your office, you might be convinced by the fact that phones and keyboards contain more germs than toilets. Your average office telephone harbours around ten thousand microbes per square centimetre – four hundred times more than a lavatory seat.* Makes you think, doesn't it? If you spend your entire working life in an office environment, the chances are you'll contract Legionnaire's Disease by the time you're fifty.**

---

* Based on research by the University of Arizona.
** Based on supposition. But it's probably true.

Few men ever drop dead from overwork, but many curl up and die because of undersatisfaction.

Sydney J. Harris

True Office Stories: Sick Offices

Staff began to notice that there seemed to be a high incidence of sickness in their office building in Washington DC. One worker became convinced that the office was causing the sickness, and went to the extreme of keeping sterilized clothes in a special fridge in her office, which she asked visitors to change into after washing with antibacterial soap. In 1997, nineteen of the office employees took the managers of the building to court, alleging that they had been brain-damaged by breathing the air inside the office, and claiming $40 million dollars in compensation. The office where the claimants worked was none other than the Environmental Protection Agency, an organization whose job was to ensure public safety from environmental illnesses. The building was found to have indoor surfaces painted with toxic outdoor paint, fungus in the ventilation system, and chemical-soaked carpeting capable of killing mice within three hours.

Sickies

It's amazing that so many of us clamour for jobs in these hellish conditions. It's only fair that you should take your revenge on this damaging environment by taking the odd sick day when you're feeling perfectly all right. Take a trip to the seaside and breathe some fresh air, safe in the knowledge that you are not inhaling your colleagues' virus-laden emissions.

Office workers never admit to taking sickies, even to colleagues who are close friends. The consequences of being caught out in a sickie are, of course, severe: it does qualify as a sackable offence, after all. But this lack of candour even among friends is further evidence of the atmosphere of fear and suspicion which is rife in office environments. Remember, everyone has taken a sickie at some time in their life.

If you want your 'sickness' to be believed, you'll need to try a bit harder than the usual 'cold' or 'upset stomach' – 'tonsillitis', 'gastroenteritis' and 'lumbago' carry more weight because they imply that at some point your symptoms have been diagnosed by a real doctor. It's always a good idea to establish that you suffer from migraines shortly after starting a new job – perhaps by mentioning to your colleagues that you suffered from one over the weekend – as this will entitle you to several free holidays a year. If you are going for a cold- or flu-related excuse, be bold: you are more likely to be believed if you take more than one day. Do beware of making your sickness excuses too ridiculous, however: no one will believe '24-hour diphtheria' or 'mild typhoid'.

Grim Offices

Offices can be attractive and well-equipped, with tinkling fountains in reception, healthy green foliage throughout the building and plenty of light and space for everyone. However, most offices fall somewhere between Newgate prison *circa* 1856 and a dingy bedsit. Instead of fountains and greenery there's a leaking tap in the toilets and a dead spider plant. There is no doubt that the physical office environment can horribly depressing, for a variety of reasons:

- Location: offices on light industrial estates or anywhere with no easy access to shops or green spaces mean that there is no getting away from the office during your lunch-break – no opportunity for decent sandwiches or retail therapy either.
- Noise: if your office is next to a busy road, you'll learn to filter out the noise after a while, but the air quality will be so appalling that it will gradually sap your health and strength. If the noise comes from a building site, for the duration of the build you will be driven out of your mind by intermittent drilling.
- Poor and dingy facilities: peeling paint, scarred and broken office furniture, leaking and smelly toilets, kitchens last updated in 1978 – all these things combine and add to the sum of your personal office misery.
- Poor equipment: if your windows don't open, the temperature is always either too hot or too cold, or the blinds don't work, forcing you to wear sunglasses to view your monitor, you will already know that seemingly low-level irritations of this kind can make you inwardly boil with rage. Over time, as you begin to realize that your requests

> *In order that people may be happy in their work, these three things are needed: They must be fit for it; they must not do too much of it; and they must have a sense of success in it.*
> **John Ruskin**

for repairs will be ignored until hell freezes over, your rage will be replaced with grim acceptance and you will resort to attempting repairs yourself. It's for this reason that in many offices there are strange cardboard constructions instead of blinds, cushions to compensate for badly designed office chairs, and piles of clothing and various fans and heaters to allow for the vagaries of the air-conditioning system.

* Infestation: it's not uncommon for office buildings to be infested with insects or rodents. Because the creatures only venture out when office workers aren't around, nothing gets done about it. The building management company will probably be aware of the problem but not want the bother of tackling it. If there's a high incidence of (genuine) stomach upsets among staff in your office, you might find that this is the reason.

 True Office Stories: Safety at Work

In 1987 staff at the Health and Safety Executive in Notting Hill went on strike because the offices were unsafe (the union spokesman described them as a 'death trap'). Improvements were eventually made, but during the building work some scaffolding collapsed and broke through a glass roof on to an office worker's desk.

> *If you think your boss is stupid, remember: you wouldn't have a job if he was any smarter.*
>
> **Albert A. Grant**

It's amazing but true that companies embark on ludicrously expensive rebranding, or a piece of sculpture that nobody likes, while their staff are trying to work in an office that resembles a rundown and badly equipped bed-and-breakfast.

Open-Plan Hell

Most people work in open-plan offices, often with partitions pathetically marking territory (otherwise known as a cube farm). There are many dreadful things about life in an open-plan office:

- Personal calls overheard by rest of office
- Difficult work calls also overheard by rest of office
- No door – people think they can bother you whenever they like
- Distracting noises – see below
- Proximity to colleagues – see below

How to be an Especially Annoying Open-Plan Office Worker

- Receive many phone calls on your personal mobile. Make sure the sound is set as loud as possible, and that the ring tone is as annoying as possible – Christmas-time presents boundless opportunities for this. Always leave the phone to ring for a good while before answering. Better still, always leave it on your desk while you're away from it without turning it off, so that colleagues are treated to several minutes of your annoying, loud ring tone.

- Hum, sing or whistle to yourself – not so loudly that people will be forced to complain but just at the level where people don't feel quite able to mention it. They will slowly be driven mad.
- Regularly use the speakerphone.
- Eat audibly and often. Fish is a good choice as its smell tends to linger for hours.
- Encroach on to your nearest co-worker's desk. This could be just a trade magazine or small pile of paperwork at first, but can build into several square feet relatively quickly. Mark your new territory with an in-tray and guard it jealously.
- Never leave your desk to get someone's attention – shout at them.
- Give a running commentary on what you are doing as often as possible – the more boring and pointless the better.
- Swear viciously at your computer every ten minutes or so.
- Listen to music on your computer. Again, keep it turned down low so that colleagues will feel unjustified in asking you to turn it off.
- Talk unnecessarily loudly.
- Steal co-workers' office equipment.

You're bound to have to put up with at least two or three of these on a regular basis. Open-plan offices are indeed hell. So it's a good idea to take as many measures as possible to try to lessen their life-draining effect:

1. You need to be able to see people before they see you – never let them creep up on you. Position your desk accordingly, otherwise your working hours will be punctuated by a series of unpleasant surprises.
2. Make sure your computer screen is not easily visible to anyone but yourself. For obvious reasons. (Also note that your monitor should face away from any windows, otherwise you will slowly be driven mad by glare.)
3. Use props such as plants to hide behind. You might be able to fool yourself that you have some kind of privacy. This is particularly important if you have an Offensive Co-worker in your line of vision (see page 130).

See also page 44 for tips on how to turn your open-plan area into a real office.

Call Centres: The Most Hellish Office Job of All

Call centres deserve a special mention because they represent a circle of office hell all of their own. It's hard to imagine a worse office job, and few call centre workers find they can stand working in them for more than a few months. This is because call centre jobs exist mainly to take the rap for companies' poor customer service and bad practice, and hence every employee is likely to be shouted at by outraged customers at least once an hour. Any office job which involves contact with the general public can be hellish, since the general public is, by and large, unreasonable and unpleasant and prone to venting pent-up rage by shouting at anyone they consider unlikely to be able to shout back. In call centres, customer rage is made worse by the interminable telephone queues in which callers are kept before the hapless call centre operator finally gets to them. These queues can reach earth-girdling proportions despite the fact that workers are monitored closely in terms of the length of their calls (if they go beyond the optimium time spent on one call they are reprimanded).

Workers also undergo timed visits to the toilet and very strictly timed tea-breaks, so that any form of slacking is rendered impossible. All of this monitoring, of course, serves to make the job even less bearable than it would be if the ranting customers were the only unpleasant aspect. Unsurprisingly, call centres tend to exist either where labour is very cheap indeed and the centre can offer better wages than most other employers, or where there is a very limited employment of any kind.

Office Party Hell

Years of commuting to work, loyal service, unpaid extra hours, working lunches and professional excellence are rewarded by many companies with three unpleasant dinner courses and a bottle of cheap wine. Sometimes public humiliation is actually prearranged on these occasions, perhaps in the form of a karaoke machine. But usually it's left to the staff to provide their own, based on large quantities of alcohol and inedible food.

Any form of organized office socializing is hell because, whatever management say, no one can relax for a second: the struggle for power is as fierce in a social environment as it is in the office itself. There are different levels of office party:

1. **Client parties**

   Obviously, these are not given for the benefit of the staff. Employees of the company are not there to enjoy themselves, and they might be specifically told this. The point of the party is to impress the clients, ply them with drink and canapés and show them what charming, happy people work for the company. Strict rules of behaviour might be set explicitly, depending on how far employees are trusted to behave themselves. Thinking of interesting things to say to complete strangers while being scrutinized by your boss can make for an excruciating evening.

He is sometimes slave who should be master; and sometimes master who should be slave.
   Cicero

 True Office Party Tales 1

At a party given for the authors, illustrators and agents of a children's publisher, nothing was left to chance. An email to staff issued instructions for mingling with guests and making sure no one was left alone or without a drink, and specifically warned employees that they were not to see the event as an opportunity to have a good time and should be very careful about the number of alcoholic drinks they consumed. Meticulous preparations were made at a prestigious venue, and the publishing company even went so far as to designate a group of young employees to begin the dancing at an appointed hour.

These provisions made it all the more surprising that one member of staff (let's call her Camilla) arrived at the venue and proceeded to get unspeakably drunk in a very short space of time. Before long she was reeling about, loudly complaining about her boss to anyone who would listen (even, at one point, to her boss), and periodically cornering unsuspecting authors and illustrators to tell them what a dreadful company they were working for. People involved in making children's books tend to be nice, fairly posh women in cardigans, so when Camilla began asking if they had any drugs on them, they became slightly alarmed. Camilla eventually had to be escorted from the building.

2. Company celebrations

These are almost but not quite as difficult as client parties. The focus is on celebrating the company, perhaps on an anniversary, so you still can't see the party as a simple excuse to get drunk at someone else's expense. Instead of thinking of interesting things to say to clients you've never met, you have to think of interesting things to say to the people who control your salary. There will be rousing speeches, and you will be expected to display loyalty to the company by cheering loudly (possibly even whooping) and talking about company achievements.

3. Christmas parties

Christmas parties are supposed to be for employees to have a good time without having to worry about clients or work – it's a purely social occasion, and the usual constraints of the office hierarchy are removed. Everyone will have a great time! This is, of course, nonsense. For a start, you're having to spend extra time with your colleagues. And of course the hierarchy still exists, you just have to pretend it doesn't. Office politicians see office parties as a golden opportunity for furthering their careers and flagrant brown-nosing ensues. If there's an opportunity to introduce themselves to senior management they will grasp it with both hands, all of which can be stomach-turning to witness. You can be sure that your boss will notice and make a swift judgement on anything you do. If you get drunk and snog someone, everyone will notice.

> *Why should we be in such desperate haste to succeed, and in such desperate enterprises? If a man does not keep pace with his companions, perhaps it is because he hears a different drummer.*
> **Henry David Thoreau**

You might think that the minefield of the Christmas party is best avoided, but you can't get out of them unless you really don't care about your promotion prospects.

Office Party Dos and Don'ts:

Don't:
- ask for a pay rise
- resign
- dance in a really stupid way
- take off any of your clothes
- punch anyone
- sing
- start any sentence with 'Do you want to know what I really think?'

Do:
- leave before there's any danger of bad behaviour, perhaps with a select band of like-minded colleagues (but be careful not to leave *too* soon)
- keep away from any mistletoe
- behave conservatively at all times
- keep away from anyone you fancy
- try not to become unspeakably drunk

> *Some slaves are scoured to their work by whips, others by their restlessness and ambition.*
>
> **John Ruskin**

True Office Party Tales 2

Maude* was offered a job at a law firm shortly before Christmas. In a spirit of friendliness, she was asked along to the office Christmas party even though she wouldn't start the job until January. You can imagine the anxiety created by this situation: if she made up an excuse, she might be seen as unfriendly and ungrateful; if she went to the party, she wouldn't know anyone at all, a social situation that is bad enough at the best of times, but when this is the first meeting with your future workmates it is hand-wringingly stressful. The possibility of having a good time was slim, but Maude decided that she should go.

The day after the party Maude woke up to a horrifying but dim memory: she had gone to the party and drunk so much that she ended up draped over the managing director, who was not wearing an encouraging expression as she propositioned him with an astounding lack of subtlety. She even remembered a small struggle to get away – but she had had the upper hand and had managed to restrain him. Even more dreadful, there were at least six witnesses who had clearly heard the whole thing and were looking on in disbelief. Perhaps surprisingly, Maude overcame her embarrassment and did start the job in January, but was asked to leave on her arrival.

* made-up name

The best thing about office parties is the possibility of senior management becoming unspeakably drunk and embarrassing themselves hideously. (Though their enormous egos will no doubt allow them to wake up the next morning and remember it all as a humorous incident that has made them even more popular with their staff.) If you're lucky, the head of the company might be so worried about making a speech that he or she will gulp down huge quantities of alcohol, throw away or lose their notes and then slur their way through an embarrassing series of personal anecdotes. But more likely is the unattractive but hilariously funny phenomenon of drunken dancing, senior-management style.

Office Romances

Office parties can all too often lead to office romances. They rarely end well. Here are ten reasons to avoid them:

1. You might think you can conceal your office relationship, but you can't. Everyone will know about it and snigger at you.
2. What seems like a beautiful office romance at 10:30 in the pub when you've been drinking since 5:30 on an empty stomach will seem like a very bad idea at 9:30 the next morning when you both arrive for work horrifically embarrassed.

> *The true way to render ourselves happy is to love and work and find in it our pleasure.*
>
> **Francoise de Motteville**

3. In the first flush of romance, you might be tempted by in-office snogging, or even by staying after hours and having sex on the photocopier. Please try to control these urges, for the good of all.

4. You might also be tempted to simper during meetings attended by both you and your girlfriend/boyfriend. Gradually, colleagues will start to hatch plots against you because of your insufferable behaviour.

5. If your office romance is with someone above you or below you in the hierarchy, this will cause untold problems. You will either be accused of giving preferential treatment or of receiving it.

6. You already spend an unhealthy amount of time thinking about the office. Since it is one of the things you have in common with your boyfriend/girlfriend, this can only increase.

7. It's always a bad idea to have a relationship with someone who can either a) monitor your internet access, email, etc.; b) refuse your expense claim forms; c) influence your salary or promotion – for obvious reasons.

8. If you already spend eight hours a day with your girlfriend or boyfriend, you will begin to resent seeing them in the evenings and at weekends as well.

9. You might be tempted to send sexually explicit emails to your office heart-throb on the company system. If you give in to temptation and hear the entire IT department laughing like hyenas, you'll know why.

> *I'm famous for my motivational skills. Everyone always says they have to work a lot harder when I'm around.*
> **Homer Simpson, *The Simpsons***

10. When you split up everyone in the office will know about it and you will be forced to see your ex every day. You might even have to work with them directly.

Corporate Insanity

Corporate insanity can be vaguely defined as how seriously the company takes itself, and how far its employees are prepared to toe the corporate line. Different offices suffer from different levels of corporate insanity and some are far worse than others. In order to gauge the madness of your office environment, ask yourself the following questions:

- Is there a corporate mission statement?
- Do the majority of your colleagues regularly use management-speak?
- Have you ever attended a large meeting solely about the company logo?
- Have you ever attended a large meeting solely about your feelings about the meeting about the company logo?
- Are motivational posters in evidence throughout the office?
- Do employees ever whoop and/or give one another high fives?
- Do you need 'core competencies' or 'proficiencies' in order to do your job?
- Do job titles sound as though they've been made up from the Job Title Fabricator on page 39?

> *I think God is using this company as a vehicle. I'm trying to take the beautiful creatures He created and help them reach down within themselves to bring out all the ability He gave them.*
> **Mary Kay Ash, founder of Mary Kay Cosmetics**

If you've answered yes to all of the above, it's going to be extremely difficult to remain sane. The only answer is to poke fun at all aspects of corporate nonsense, seek out like-minded colleagues and look for another job.

Motivation, Motivation, Motivation

If your company spends time and money on motivational weekends quadbiking just outside Birmingham in order to improve teamwork and productivity, or there are regular courses on 'motivational skills', something is very wrong. This tends to be what companies do instead of providing a pleasant working environment, fair working hours, managers who offer support and advice, proper training and decent salaries. Few companies realize that no one really needs motivating if they're doing a job they enjoy in return for a fair wage.

Motivational posters are a sure sign of corporate insanity. Who, for example, would do a better job as a result of seeing the following toe-curling phrases emblazoned across posters with images of dolphins or rowing teams:

Success: *Some people succeed because they are destined to, but most succeed because they are determined to.*

Goals: *What the mind can conceive and believe, it can achieve.*

Possibilities: *The only way to discover the limits of the possible is to go beyond them into the impossible.*

Dare: *Great results require ambitions.*

As you feel your spirit being drained by the demands your power-crazed sadist of a boss in a ludicrously overworked and underpaid job, looking up and seeing a motivational poster with a picture of a snowboarder and the words *Life's only limitations are the ones we make* underneath it is bound to make you feel so much better. You'll probably feel motivated to do some unpaid overtime.

Mission Statements

Senior management will spend several days – or even weeks – formulating mission statements consisting of meaningless management-speak nonsense. They might find they need to go on an expensive country retreat together in order to fully identify what the company stands for. It would probably take you a couple of hours on a bad day to come up with this drivel.

> *Plans are only good intentions unless they immediately degenerate into hard work.*
>
> **Peter Drucker**

How to Formulate Your Mission Statement

Your mission statement should communicate the company's 'business vision'. This means defining your 'core values', 'core purpose' and 'visionary goals'.

Core values

Whatever line of business you're in, whether public or private sector, whether the company makes car tyres or provides a management consultancy service, it doesn't matter. Simply choose from this list of possible core values:

Innovation
Excellent customer service
Creativity
Social responsibility (though this will depend on the
    company: you might decide it's better not to draw
    attention to it)
Integrity
Quality

You could use all of them if you like, or add new ones. Each 'core value' will need a little bit of explanation. For example:

Innovation: *We seek to nurture innovation at all levels of our business in order to enhance and grow our products and customer service.*

> *A tremendous number of people in America work very hard at some-thing that bores them. Even a rich man thinks he has to go down to the office every day. Not because he likes it but because he can't think of anything else to do.*
>   W. H. Auden

 True Office Tales: Corporate Nonsense

From the Lake Geneva Forum website: 'Our challenge: Providing a neutral platform of discourse to capture, explore and integrate a systems view of things in order to unleash and bring together the relative potential of the dominant global institutions in an atmosphere of trust for steering our political, economical, scientific and cultural values and beliefs towards a greater sense of global social and ecological responsibility and thereby create new and positive outcomes for cross culture problem and conflict resolution.'

Core purpose

The 'core purpose' of any company is obviously to make money. That's capitalism for you. Don't say this, though. Instead, focus on how profit is made – which I think you'll find is by empowering your clients to reach their objectives, and by offering them greater choice of innovative, creative product.

Visionary Goals

One of your goals might be to reach a quantifiable target – to sell 10,000 of your product per week, for example.

You might also want to overtake a specific competitor, or to increase your product base.

Now simply sum up all of the above in a meaningless mission statement. For example:

Our aim is to create innovative, outstanding product, empowering our client base through greater choice and excellent customer service, and continuing our position as market leaders on a going forward basis.

 True Office Tales: Corporate Sun-tan

Not all written corporate insanity uses this type of formula and language. Some of it is much more bizarre. On its website, Joe Brown's Adventure Clothing and Accessories describes itself: 'If you can imagine at the end of the day, coming out of the sea with salty hair and a tightish sun-tanned face and walking into a beach bar surrounded by people having a good time with music playing and laughter, then if you could bottle up that feeling – that's the essence of our company.'

Vision Statements

Lots of companies have a separate 'vision statement' as well as a mission statement. This might be a very long-term goal, possibly one that's unattainable – like 'world domination', for example. Make sure yours is something suitably grand. Perhaps your company should seek to revolutionize the industry in some way, or ensure that everyone in the Western world is familiar with your brand name.

Spreading the Word

Now you need to cascade your mission statement down through the company hierarchy. It's vital that each employee is familiar with the company's core values, core purpose and business vision. This will help to motivate them. You'll need to have a series of meetings on the subject, with accompanying documentation. Since you've spent so much time and effort, you might like to have the mission statement, vision statement, core values, etc. leather-bound into an attractive little booklet and distributed to employees free of charge. Staff will feel honoured and grateful for this expensive gift.

It would be a waste of time formulating your mission statement and making your staff aware of it if employees are not going to put the company's core values into practice. Managers will need to ensure that they are – perhaps by asking them to complete a 25-page questionnaire, and having further meetings to discuss the results. Another way of ensuring key messages are kept alive might be to have posters made that express key messages. These will probably sit very well alongside the other motivational posters in the office.

Rebranding

Mission statements are often formulated as a result of a rebranding – which itself might be prompted by a company anniversary or similar. Rebrandings are often particularly difficult for the majority of staff to swallow, because everyone knows that the cost of it is monumental while the benefits of using a slightly different typeface are debatable and very difficult to quantify anyway.

Usually, the company rebranding is outsourced to a specialist consultancy (which is why so many company logos look similar in style). After several months and possibly several million pounds, staff are presented with the same company name but in aquamarine and lower-case letters, or alternatively a completely different company name which will undoubtedly sound ridiculous (recent real-life examples include Consignia, Accenture and, perhaps most risible, Monday). If your Managing Director or equivalent asks you what you think of the new company logo, it's best not to utter heartfelt curses but to think of something positive to say – for example, if the logo has changed from black and white to colour, it's presenting a more fun, lively

> *It is better to have loafed and lost than never to have loafed at all.*
> **James Thurber**

image; if it's the other way around, it's achieved more suitable gravitas.

 True Office Tales: Office Freedom

Corporate insanity can take many forms. In 1993 the boss of a US advertising agency decided to free his employees' minds ... by dispensing with desks, filing cabinets and even paper. The idea was that staff would be emancipated by sitting on sofas and wandering about freely instead of having to keep records and files (no paper was allowed). There were special rooms for meetings, also equipped with comfy seating.

Not surprisingly, staff found it very difficult to work under these conditions. Instead of keeping necessary files and records in a desk inside the office, many of them began using their cars instead of a desk, and had to go out to the car park when they needed to refer to something on paper. Some built makeshift desks in the meeting rooms.

Eventually, the company was bought by a rival with more traditional ideas, and staff reverted to normal office life.

Vanity Publishing

An unusual extra to a rebranding or company anniversary celebration is for the company to publish its own book. A hardback, full-colour, coffee-table-style history of the company is given to every employee. Obviously, no one in their right mind would actually read it and everyone wonders what they're supposed to do with it. While most people can see the funny side of having the company's founder lauded as a visionary genius in the cut-and-thrust world of paperclips, every employee is inwardly seething at the considerable cost of this pointless venture, which (in addition to the rebranding and senior management's time and hotel bill), is presumably in lieu of a payrise.

Escape from Office Hell

Bad bosses, office politics, presentations, meetings, corporate nonsense, open-plan offices – escape is necessary. Luckily there are several different ways of making office hell slightly more bearable. Obviously, you must carefully gauge exactly how much slacking you can get away with – someone is almost bound to notice if you do absolutely nothing. If you do the kind of job which is hard to quantify (such as managing people) you will find you are able to waste company time far more effectively than otherwise.

Slacking in the Office

All office workers spend a portion of their time at the office untroubled by actual work. If they didn't they would probably

> *If at first you don't succeed, remove all evidence you ever tried.*
> **Anonymous**

go mad. But champion slackers (everyone who works in an office knows at least one of these – see page 136) manage to create a very high ratio between the amount of time spent at work and the amount of time spent working.

Slacking in the office can be achieved in various ways:

The Internet

The internet is the slacker's friend. As long as people can't creep up on you and see that what you are labouring over so intently is your online Sainsbury's shopping, it is very easy to disguise as real work emailing friends, playing games, shopping, house-hunting, pursuing hobbies, participating in discussion groups, researching holiday destinations and looking at pornography. However, see page 112 for some words of caution on internet use.

Chatting

If your pals at work have their own offices, this is made very easy indeed: your boss won't know that you were in a colleague's office for two hours talking about what you did at the weekend. If the office is open-plan, wasting time in idle chatter can be more difficult. You will need to develop a way of speaking that is inaudible to the casual observer and yet can't be categorized as whispering. Some people are able to while away entire days, or even weeks in large offices, simply by visiting acquaintances throughout the office. Tea-making provides a good opportunity for chatting, especially if the kitchen has a closable door.

> *It is impossible to enjoy idling thoroughly unless one has plenty of work to do.*
>
> **Jerome K. Jerome**

Smoking

Fast becoming a thing of the past, smoking still provides opportunities for chatting to other people or just staring into space as you lurk outside the office building. Some offices have 'smoking rooms', which provide great opportunities for gossiping with fellow workers in relative comfort (and the smoking room provides the perfect place to bitch about anyone who is a non-smoker, of course). If your company has a smoking room, you might want to consider taking up the habit. It's not uncommon for smoking slackers to remain in smoking rooms for hours at a time, turning a bilious shade of yellow as a result.

Long Lunch Hours

Unless your office is very rigid about when staff should take their lunch hours (in which case, bad luck), it's quite simple to extend your lunch-break far beyond the customary hour. Half an hour either side of the usual lunch slot – between one and two o'clock – won't be noticed. Happily, this means that you can regularly take two-hour-long lunch breaks – between half past twelve and half past two – if you feel like it.

Coming in Late and Sloping off Early

Of course there is a limit to how much of this you can get away with. If you are unfortunate enough to have to sign in and out in some way, it will be impossible. Lateness excuses are easy to come up with – public transport is always to blame. But you will need to think hard to provide a decent excuse for early departure – a meeting outside the office, for example, as long as you're sure no one will check.

There are also many opportunities for slacking outside the office:

Training Courses

If you've used your performance appraisal wisely (see page 57) you should have amassed plenty of these. As long as they're not residential (when you run the risk of being stuck in a living hell surrounded by morons twenty-four hours a day), training courses are your chance to have a nice little break from the office. Training companies know that most people won't recommend their course if a) the trainer is a complete git; or b) if the course is in any way taxing. So courses are run by pleasant, smiling people who make little jokes and are extremely nice to everyone (perhaps they spend their non-teaching time in primal scream therapy), and attainment targets are set so low that a woodlouse could hurdle them. Relax and unwind as you enjoy a nice short day not having to think very hard, with regular breaks for tea. You even get biscuits.

The number one sign you have nothing to do at work: The 4th Division of Paperclips has overrun the Pushpin Infantry and General White-Out has called for a new skirmish.

Fred Barling

Trips

You might find you need to do 'research' outside of the office. This can be as simple as going shopping for products from other companies for comparison with the products your own company makes – you have to admit, it sounds perfectly reasonable, and yet the opportunity for slacking is obvious. See if you can instigate 'comp shopping' if your company doesn't already it do it.

Visiting trade fairs is another good excuse for a trip away from the office for a bit of much-needed relaxation. If these can be abroad then so much the better, especially if you have friends in foreign countries where the trade fairs are. Obviously you must ensure you go alone, so that there's no one to check up on what you are doing.

Working From Home

You might try to persuade your employer to allow you to work from home on a permanent basis. Most companies are not keen on this idea, even though it's very easy to accomplish. They will tell you that this is because personal contact with colleagues is vitally important, your physical presence in meetings is essential, and being able to have impromptu face-to-face discussions with you is key to the functioning of the entire company. The real reason is that they know the opportunities for slacking are legion.

It's true that when you work from home, everything – even the ironing – seems far more attractive than doing any work. It is almost impossible to resist the strange allure of housework and most home workers discover that they can't do any work until the entire home is vacuumed, surfaces polished, washing-up done, clothes washed and dried, furniture reorganized, chimney swept, garden tidied and perhaps landscaped – by which time it's too late to do anything else.

The advantages of working from home are that a) commuting is eliminated; b) there's no dress code; c) you'll never have to spend your 'leisure time' doing any housework; and d) there are endless opportunities for slacking without fear of being caught. The one disadvantage is that you might find you crave human contact and start bothering neighbours, shop assistants and random passers-by. However, since your company is unlikely to allow you to work from home all the time, this probably won't be a problem. In most office jobs, it's possible to invent reasons for the odd day working from home, particularly if you work in an open-plan office. If there are aspects of your job that require close concentration, your boss is unlikely to feel able to turn you down, much though he or she would like to.

Office technology should be a tool to help people do their jobs better and more efficiently, and yet all too often it is a source of frustration and stress. If the computers themselves weren't enough, there's the technical staff (more on them later), the insanely complicated company systems and the problematic software.

Email and its Many Pitfalls

Email is a wonderful thing. If you can remember the days before it arrived, you will also recall the daily hundredweight of envelopes that had to be addressed and posted, the unreadable faxes with barely recognizable images, having to print out and post long documents, and the impossibility of chatting to friends for extended periods during working hours completely unobserved. However, email comes with its problems and pitfalls too:

Rude Emails and the 'Reply to All' Button

It's not that easy to be very rude to someone over the phone, by letter or in person – you have to be really annoyed for that to happen. However, email almost seems to incite rudeness. How many of us have begun an insulting or inflamatory response only to see sense halfway through – or send the email then immediately regret telling the head of Human Resources that he's 'spouting nonsense' (even though he almost certainly is).

At some point in your office career, you will compose a witty, sharp, incredibly insulting email in response to one you have received, fully intending to send it. But instead of sending it to the one person on the list of recipients who would share your views, you will hit the Reply to All button by mistake. Beware of this: describing your colleagues as 'slack-jawed ruminants' and the Managing Director as 'that gibbering fool' is probably a sackable offence. Be on your guard – this is an email accident waiting to happen.

Recalling emails is possible, depending on what system is set up in your office. But it's probably best not to try. Workers in one office were surprised to receive an insane tirade addressed to the entire company from the (admittedly bonkers) office manager, then even more surprised, and amused, to receive it again with a notice from the email system informing everyone that 'the email below has been recalled by the sender'.

> *Computers make it easier to do a lot of things, but most of the things they make it easier to do don't need to be done.*
>
> **Andy Rooney**

Everyone-emails

Some people are fond of sending out a 'newsletter' at Christmas-time, detailing their family's ups and downs throughout the year, and generally expressing how great the sender and his or her family are. They don't seem to realize that nobody cares whether Joanne passed her A Levels, or that they are almost universally loathed.

These same people work in offices and are responsible for all those long, annoying and unnecessary emails which are sent to everyone in the company and designed to express just how great the sender (and maybe his or her team) is. In fact, there are many more of these people than Christmas newsletter senders – the office environment seems to encourage people to give in to these urges. They hope that by generating thousands of words of management-speak singing their own praises people will be impressed, congratulate them on their achievements and bestow promotions and pay rises. To some extent, this must work: notice that these emails are always sent by people from the higher echelons of management. Colleagues feel they have to read these intensely irritating documents just in case, buried somewhere in the middle of page three, there is some vital piece of information. But there seldom is.

The other kind of everyone-emails that drive us all mad are the lost-property variety ('a pair of gloves has been found in the ladies toilet …'). Admittedly, sometimes they can be quite funny, depending on the incongruity of the item and where it was found – Y-fronts in reception, a packed lunch in a toilet cistern and a pair of trousers neatly folded

---

on the fire escape have all been known. Office managers
are fond of sending irritating everyone-emails with instructions or advice on office facilities – a recent favourite was,
'Please don't use more toilet paper than is absolutely
necessary'.

Receiving Incriminating Emails

You can be completely innocent of any wrongdoing and still
get into serious trouble because of email. Everyone knows at
least one person who thinks emailing disgusting, preferably
sexual, images is very funny. (If you are male and under 35,
this will probably apply to you and most of your friends.)
Many people have had to take the consequences of receiving something utterly vile (perhaps with accompanying
sound effects) and opening it just as the boss approaches
their desk. Because of this, the importance of the position
of your desk and monitor cannot be emphasized enough. It's
probably a good idea to turn off the sound on your
computer, too.

Sending Incriminating Emails

If you're considering sending an email to a trusted colleague
complaining bitterly about your boss, or telling a friend
outside the office that you took a sickie yesterday, think
again. For those who don't realize: the whole of the IT
department looks at any personal emails you send and
laughs at your indiscretions and personal information. Or at
least they can if they feel like it. If you've incurred the wrath
of someone high up in the company to the extent that they

> *Computers are useless. They can only give you answers.*
> **Pablo Picasso**

would like to sack you, they might well enlist the help of the IT department and look for a sackable offence among your email. Deleting anything incriminating won't work either – back-up files are kept for years. Never forget that your computer and email account is not yours but the company's. If you're going to send incriminating emails from the office, make sure you do it on your personal account.

 True Office Tales: Embarrassing Email

In December 2000, Claire Swires sent an email to a boyfriend's office email address (at a London law firm) which, rather unwisely, praised the taste and quality of one of his bodily fluids. The boyfriend, Bradley Chait, was desperate to impress and male, so he forwarded Claire's praises to six of his colleagues. Claire used to work for the same company as Bradley so the email counted as office gossip as well as being mildly amusing: within an hour the email had made its way around most of the City of London. The email grew as it continued on its way, gathering comments from each person forwarding it. Within three days it had travelled the world and become so famous that the press started besieging Claire's parents' home in southern England.

The City law firm, Norton Rose, also found out about it. They decided that they didn't want their company's name endorsing the emissions of a member of staff, and sacked Bradley and several of his colleagues.

The IT department will also periodically monitor your internet use, so if you've ever logged on to a web address you'd rather they didn't find out about, you can be sure that they already have. The fact that you were looking at it for several hours means excuses such as 'it was a mistake – I was doing research' won't cut any ice. Take heed of the Dutch office worker whose porn download was responsible for all the computers in his department crashing. Of course, a cursory investigation found that he was responsible within minutes.

Email: the Thief of Time

Does email really save time? No doubt you arrive in the office every day to an inbox brimming with unread emails, and often the entire working day is spent trying to keep the email inbox under control. When left untamed it can expand with astonishing speed, each email breeding yet more until eventually you are faced with the task of spending all your time for several days (or even weeks in extreme cases) coaxing it back to manageable proportions.

The trouble is that email is the lazy person's dream come true since they don't even have to move or open their mouths in order to be seen to work. Email provides countless opportunities to attempt to pass the buck by sending vague and unclear emails instead of actually doing anything. Also, staff who aren't confident about what they're doing will often copy in as many of their colleagues as possible to their email correspondence. All of which means your inbox will be littered with puzzling and confusing emails from idle or incompetent colleagues as well as countless emails you've been copied into by people hoping to cover their backs if something goes wrong. Then there are the 'Aren't I great?' newsletters, the ones informing you that a lady's thong has been found in Accounts, the ones about the photocopier on the second floor – is it any wonder people crack and end up sending vicious hate mail to their colleagues?

The Scary IT Department

If you don't work in IT, the chances are you will see IT staff as socially inept, technology-obsessed, anally-retentive people who play a lot of role-play computer games. If you do work in IT, even you will have to admit that this is at least partly true. However, the higher up the management structure you go, the less it's true: lack of technical knowledge is actually a mark of seniority in IT departments. Those right at the top have by far the best equipment but are incapable of using it.

Many non-IT people are scared of the office's technical staff, hesitating before calling the helpdesk and, once called, hoping that their entire harddrive has been wiped by a mystery technical glitch rather than that the smallest

> *If you touch any key, our software will lock up. Call us and we'll blame it on Microsoft.*
> **Scott Adams,** *Dilbert*

problem should arise from anything they've done. The fear is that the IT person will think you are an idiot – which for some reason is very scary.

There's no doubt that some office technology systems are over-complicated and badly designed and take a lot of training to fully understand. They can be a source of bitter annoyance and frustration and result in many wasted hours. Often

---

 True Office Tales: Flashing Lights are Impressive

Because so many people are impressed by technical knowledge (or the semblance of it), IT staff have many opportunities for slacking. For example, the singer Elvis Costello was a computer operator in the 1970s. He once said, 'In the 70s, operating a computer was the ultimate bluffer's job. You wore a white lab coat and people assumed you were some kind of scientist, because you had this giant machine with twinkling lights and tapes revolving.' Happily this freed him from the constraints of doing any work, and he spent his time reading the paper, writing songs and booking gigs. We may not have the lights and tape decks any more, but the same thing is still true. IT staff are well-known blaggers and many of them have barely any more technical knowledge than you do – they just count on the fact that people are impressed by flashing lights.

---

staff are never properly trained and end up making lots of unnecessary calls to the IT department, who think the systems are easy to understand and assume that most of the users are mentally subnormal.

The truth is that all IT staff see their non-technical colleagues as bumbling buffoons and don't care if they know it. If you phone the IT helpdesk with a problem, having first spent hours checking connections and worrying that you have done something stupid, the first response will be a weary, 'Have you left the caps lock on?' The really terrible thing is, you probably have. Did you know that the very term 'user' is in fact pejorative in IT parlance?

In every office there is one person who bucks the trend and phones the IT helpdesk on any pretext – one favourite in recent memory was 'not being able to find the "@" key'. These people do not realize that the technical staff fantasize about garrotting them with their own mouse cable.

Similarly, in every office there is one person who simply refuses to touch any form of technology. These technophobes are usually at least 105 years old and therefore probably in a position of senior management. For this reason they are humoured – sometimes to the extent of employing someone specifically to make sense of their spidery long-hand. In one office, a manager had mastered the basics of using his computer as a typewriter, but clearly hadn't quite understood. He handed a typewritten letter to a temporary secretary, asking her to 'type it up on headed paper'.

Tragic Tales of IT Bafflement

Assuming you can locate the '@' key, hearing about people who are even more technically challenged than you are can make you feel mildly better about technology, the IT Department and life in general ...

- The most famous Stupid User Story involves a helpdesk call from a woman who claimed that her computer monitor had mysteriously gone blank. The helpdesk operator went through the various different things that might have happened to cause this, checking that various cables hadn't become unplugged. After some time, the user mentioned that she was having trouble seeing something at the back of her computer because it was dark. 'Isn't there a light you can turn on?' asked the helpdesk operator. 'No, because there's been a power cut,' replied the woman. The operator suggested that she should take her computer back to the shop where she'd bought it, explaining that she was too stupid to own a computer.
- Although he had a rudimentary grasp of how to use the word-processing software, using email was beyond one user. He accumulated 500 emails in his inbox over several weeks without being able to open any of them. Realizing the depth of his ignorance, he felt too embarrassed to call the helpdesk, and he couldn't ask his

> *To err is human but to really foul things up requires a computer.*
> **Farmer's Almanac**

colleagues because they all hated him (perfectly illustrating another aspect of office hell, he'd been promoted above them and was bitterly resented). Finally, he managed slowly to learn how to at least open emails and – after some difficulty – reply to them, after many phone calls to his girlfriend.

- After a long conversation, the helpdesk operator decided to see for himself why a user kept getting an error message. All became clear: faced with a menu screen that gave three numbered choices followed by the instruction 'press the number of your choice', the user pressed 7 and, not surprisingly, got the error message. When asked, he simply explained that 7 was the number of his choice – he was doing exactly what the instruction said.

- The mouse can present problems to the uninitiated. After a very basic training session on computer use, a senior manager called over the teacher and explained that he could get his cursor to go from side to side (he demonstrated by moving his mouse from side to side on the mousepad), but couldn't seem to make it go up and down (he demonstrated by moving the mouse up and down in the air in front of the screen). At least he wasn't using it as a foot pedal, or pointing at the screen as if it were a remote control, which have also been known.

- Many helpdesks claim to have heard complaints from users that they can't find the 'any' key, having been prompted by the computer to 'press any key'.

How to Incur the Wrath of the IT Department

If you don't particularly mind losing all your work, here are a few ways to really annoy the IT staff.

- If you get a virus warning from a mate, send it to everyone in your address book.
- Refer to 'computer stuff' in a derogatory way.
- Use the words 'geek' and 'nerd'.
- Refer to computer role-playing games in a derogatory way.
- Never bother reading error messages – it's always just nonsense and a bunch of numbers.
- Send enormous documents – preferably nothing to do with work – at busy times of the day.
- Open an unknown email attachment that contains a virus.
- Say, 'Well, it didn't work when *I* did it.'
- Assume that IT staff are intimate with every aspect of every piece of software on your computer.

IT Excuses

If you've ever been baffled by technology or patronized by the helpdesk, you might be pleased to know that IT can be also be used as an excuse for not doing any work. Hurray!

Excuse 1: If the system goes down for a couple of hours and you've failed to do something, you can blame the system – even if you've had six months in which to complete your task. This excuse always works, at least on non-technical managers.

Excuse 2: The easiest and most obvious way to sabotage your computer is to gently loosen one or two cables. Complain loudly that your computer has stopped working and put in a call to IT. This will give you the perfect excuse if you've missed a deadline, but only if you work in a large company where responses to helpdesk calls take a few hours (this applies to excuses 3, 4 and 5, too). The IT person won't think this is strange, since cables become loose all the time, and it might well be the first thing he or she checks.

Excuse 3: This one entails slightly more bother, but you won't be able to use excuse number two very often without arousing suspicion: swap the fuse in your plug with one that's blown. Again, wait for IT, and make sure everyone knows you're unable to work on your important, time-sensitive document.

Excuse 4: Anything with an electric motor will probably disrupt your monitor enough to render it unusable. An electric fan on your desk is a good choice.

Excuse 5: Fiddle with the settings on your monitor so that it becomes difficult or impossible to read. This could easily have happened by accident.

The above methods of sabotage are a small-minded and petty way of secretly getting your revenge on the IT department, as well as being useful excuses.

I f you loathe going to the office every day, the main reason is probably your colleagues.

Ordinarily, you choose the people you spend your time with. You make these choices based on various personal preferences and some basic social considerations: for example, you wouldn't want to be in the company of an egomaniac who laughs at the misfortunes of others and is solely concerned with his own personal gain. And yet it's exactly this sort of person who seems to thrive in the office environment – you will probably have to spend many hours in the company of at least one. If you're unlucky you'll be sharing a desk with someone you loathe. It's a bit like a very large dysfunctional family, except that you have to spend more of your waking hours with your colleagues and you're far more likely to want to kill them than your parents.

What follows are some gross generalizations about some of the different departments (IT has already had a whole chapter to itself), plus a comprehensive range of particular office types.

Insulting Departmental Generalizations

The Human Resources Department

The very title Human Resources is unsettling. The two words seem wrong together, a bit like 'human' and 'flesh'. And the people who work in HR are very often deeply unsettling themselves – for example, lots of them think that psychometric tests are very clever and give the HR department a unique insight into other employees' personalities.

HR staff try to make up for the fact that they don't really have anything to do for most of the time by desperately trying to invent things. For example, many HR departments have managed to make a pseudo-science out of job descriptions (among other things). Most people would agree that it's a good idea to have some kind of basic job description, but few can see the advantages of one that is written exclusively in management-speak and consists of thirty-five 'competencies', each of which is subdivided into four key skill areas, none of which actually means anything. In one scientific organization with a particularly insane HR department, the scientists are known as 'knowledge workers' and their job descriptions imply that managerial skills and a willingness to be part of a team are the most important elements of their work.

Other than creating these confusing documents, the HR department is responsible for providing new employees with lots of forms about pension schemes and eye tests – no wonder they always look rushed off their feet. And another thing: have you noticed how a high proportion of HR staff have their own offices compared to other departments?

The Finance Department

Finance department staff tend to be introverted, good at IT and obsessed with spreadsheets. They also have greater opportunity than most to embezzle company funds and it's this aspect that makes them interesting – even glamorous. In one recent case, a finance department worker embezzled over £1,000 per week by the simple device of creating invoices and paying them into a bank account. After about ten months he left the company, picked up his healthy bank balance and returned to his native South Africa, never to be seen again. A reorganization of the department followed swiftly afterwards, and finance enjoyed a new respect: so *that's* why they do it.

The Marketing and Sales Department

Bill Hicks once said, 'If anyone here is in advertising or marketing, kill yourself ... You're the ruiner of all things good … you are Satan's spawn, filling the world with bile and garbage … kill yourself now.' It seems a bit extreme, granted, but which of us hasn't had similar thoughts at some time about Marketing and Sales?

The job of the Marketing and Sales department (or Sales and Marketing, depending on the background of the person in charge of it) is to hookwink customers into buying products that are very cheap to produce for very large amounts of money. Again, a whole pseudo-science has grown up in the pursuit of this aim, and there's a lot of euphemistic management-speak involved. But the truth is that people who work in the Marketing and Sales department possess only a vestigial conscience and are not to be trusted.

The Creative Department

If your office has a Creative department, it will undoubtedly be full of insufferable men with ponytails and other ego-maniacs. Everyone in the department will be unfeasibly pleased with themselves. The main reason these people are so difficult to bear is that they don't see what they do as a job, but as part of their personality – they might even refer to themselves as 'Creatives'. They consider them-selves to be immensely talented and of course you will be expected to as well (otherwise there will be tantrums). However, there is a plus side: egos are fragile, so it's easy to get your revenge on a member of the Creative depart-ment by subtly casting doubt on the brilliance of one of his or her 'concepts' (this might provoke further tantrums, but it will be worth it).

Office Types: A Field Guide

The Thruster

Scarily ambitious and confident, the Thruster would cheerfully kick away his own grandmother's Zimmer frame if he thought he could use it to help him climb up the corporate ladder. He is manipulative and knows no scruple, and is highly skilled at toadying and other forms of office politics. Sometimes, Thrusters give the impression that they are caring, friendly people. Do not be fooled: they don't care whether you live or die, and if they are being nice to you it'll only be because they think you might be useful to them in some way.

In fact, Thrusters are the most successful of all office politicians. They are often difficult to spot immediately because many of them give a good impression of reasonable, even kind people. However, it's possible to spot a Thruster by his or her reaction when thwarted, which will be one of barely suppressed rage. Disguising insincerity might also be a weak point.

Thrusters will almost certainly use management-speak to some degree, depending on whom they're talking to – they'll want to impress anyone above them in the hierarchy who uses it, of course. In some cases they might also be Whoopers, depending on the office environment. But Thrusters differ from mere Whoopers and Tigers because they are more likely to be successful and make it to senior management (in fact, the majority of senior management is made up of Thrusters).

Insane Office Managers

Generally speaking, the lower down the hierarchy the office manager is, the nicer and more reasonable she will be (they're nearly always women for some reason). But the higher up the scale, the more bonkers. The worst-case scenario is an office manager reaching director level, whereupon she will turn into a vicious harpie obsessed with toilets and milk quotas. If there is an office reorganization, or indeed if she is forced to take any action at all, beware: the Insane Office Manager will be on a very short fuse due to the pressure of having to do something other than moan about wasted teabags and the state of the fridge, and may become aggressive.

The Late Worker

This common office type stays at the office long after the end of the working day, usually due to abject insecurity. Often, Late Workers have wasted so much time during the day (telling as many colleagues as possible what time they left the office last night) that the only time available to do any work is after office hours – but they are strangely unable to make this observation themselves. They try to make sure they send at least one group email just before they leave for the night (or early morning in extreme cases), just so that everyone gets the message. It's not unusual to find that they've ordered in pizza, which is responsible for the lingering smell that will add to the Late Worker's unpopularity.

Late Workers want to succeed in the world of office politics, but fail miserably. All they get for their efforts is the reputation of a lazy slacker who eats a lot of take-aways. They don't seem to realize that turning up late for work on a regular basis is a cardinal office sin – they think they are perfectly justified to do so because they stay late, but senior managers will hate them for it. They might also be regularly late for meetings due to their woeful lack of organization, wasting other people's time and making themselves even less popular.

The Late Worker might also be a Whooper, and possibly a Management-Speaker, but if they are they'll be hopeless at it.

The Gossip

Office gossips love it when new people arrive in the company because everyone else has learned to be wary of them and never parts with any interesting information. If you're starting a new job, beware of anyone who seems very friendly and asks a lot of personal questions: your sexual history will become general knowledge within hours.

Mr (or Ms) Whiffy

There's nearly always someone in the office who does something physically repulsive, but occasionally you find an extreme case who always smells musty (at best), wears a

---

 True Office Tales: The £60,000 Fart

Goran Andervass, a Swedish computer technician, was offended by his colleague's foul-smelling fart, which he felt had been emitted in his office deliberately. Goran made his feelings known to his colleague in such an animated and vociferous way that the farter felt justified in complaining to management. Eventually, Goran lost his job over the incident. However, he felt that he had been right to vent his anger about the fart, and took the company to court – which agreed with him and paid him £60,000 in compensation. A spokesman from the Swedish Work Environment Authority said, 'If a fart is done on purpose when going into somebody's office, it is important that management takes the matter seriously.'

---

limited wardrobe of stained clothing, and has a wide variety
of disgusting habits in which they indulge freely around the
office (for example, nose-picking, belching, cleaning out
ears with a cotton bud, farting – sometimes lifting a facilitat-
ing cheek from the office chair). You can lessen the visual
effects easily enough with strategically placed plants and
office equipment, but there's not much you can do about the
noise and the smells.

The Shameless Brown-Noser

Like the Late Worker, the Shameless Brown-Noser is an
office type who desperately wants to succeed but doesn't
understand how to be a good office politician. All they
achieve with their obvious, cringe-making toadying is the
dislike of their colleagues. Brown-Nosers look up to
Thrusters with admiration and awe: in their hearts they
know they will never achieve the ruthless intelligence and
lack of scruple necessary to become a Thruster.

The Loon

Many of your colleagues will be a bit eccentric or have some
strange and/or annoying habits. Loons, however, are properly mad. Depending on the size of the company you work
for, there might well be a Loon lurking somewhere in your

office: one Loon per 50 employees is the average. Loons can come from any stratum of the office hierarchy, though it is rare to find them towards the top (the chances increase dramatically if it's a family business, however).

Of course, there are as many different types of Loon as there are different types of insanity. Here are a few examples of the disturbing behaviour they might display:

- follow colleagues about in an unsettling fashion – in extreme cases, stalking colleagues
- throw regular 'temper tantrums' involving stamping feet and shouting (usually the reserve of management Loons)
- spread bizarre and obviously made-up rumours – for example (in one recent case) that the Head of IT is moonlighting by running an escort agency, or that the CEO has impregnated all of the pregnant women in the company
- find choosing office supplies (or similar) so stressful that they have to have a lie-down afterwards

Many of them seem quite normal at first – which is presumably how they hurdled the interview process. On the other hand, perhaps the Loon *was* perfectly normal when he or she started at the company: it could be that office life has driven them insane. A sobering thought for us all.

Loons might also be Insane Office Managers (naturally), Late Workers, Crisis Monkeys, Tigers or Home-Makers.

The Whooper

Whoopers are overly enthusiastic employees who whoop like chimps when they hear of high company performance levels, see the latest company product or new logo, etc. They might also be keen high-fivers.

Different companies and departments have different whooping levels. Whooping is not typically British and remains far more unusual in Europe than in the US, but worryingly it is on the increase. Sales and Marketing departments are likely to have the highest levels but – disturbingly – it can happen anywhere. Sometimes a Whooper will have learned their whooping habits at another company, then be unable to stop themselves from whooping at a new one where whooping is highly unusual, causing embarrassment all round.

Whoopers might often also be Thrusters (if they are very confident Whoopers) or Tigers.

The Joker

Most offices have an official Joker, who is characterized by being deeply unfunny. He or she will be responsible for forwarding 'humorous' emails around the company.

The Tiger

Tigers are managers who have obviously read one too many self-help-style management books and can't stop spouting motivational nonsense. Unfortunately, they're incapable of making any of it sound convincing – usually it just sounds incredibly patronizing and/or idiotic. They will almost certainly be big on motivational group emails ('YOU can make a difference! Let's make it double the sales this month!').

Some Tigers can tip over the edge and become corporate fiends, characterized by twitching, hand-wringing and slavering. They have been driven mad because their desperate efforts to climb the greasy pole towards senior management have met with failure: to a Tiger, fruitless effort simply makes no sense because it doesn't agree with the tenets of management lore, and this may cause a short-circuit in the Tiger's brain.

Tigers have none of the aplomb and natural talents of the Thruster. They are most commonly found in sales, and they will almost definitely be Whoopers.

The Complainer

Of course, moaning about your job and the office in general is natural, and indeed necessary for good health and sanity. But there are some people who take complaining to another level. They rarely open their mouths without whining and cast a deathly pall of depression wherever they go. In extreme cases they will continue to complain about their job *years after they have left the company.*

The Home-Maker

The office environment can be grim and soulless. A few office workers over-compensate by making their office space into a home-from-home. They might start with a couple of plants and a photo, but a few months later they're surrounded by foliage, stuffed toys, posters, several different articles of clothing and perhaps a small chest of drawers. They might start buying their own stationery and other office supplies in the interests of co-ordination: somewhere along the line it has become vitally important to the Home-Maker that the mouse mat and coffee mug are the same colour.

It goes without saying that extreme examples of Home-Makers might also be Loons.

The Crisis Monkey

Some people have a poorly developed sense of proportion and see everything as hugely important. A minor problem for anyone else is a huge crisis for Crisis Monkeys. They will look as though they haven't slept in weeks and might display

Some workers are trying to make both weekends meet.
Anonymous

 True Office Tales: Champion Slacking

Two real examples demonstrate the subdivisions of Champion Slacker. Joe was an electrical engineer who a) took several weeks of sick leave when he was perfectly healthy, claiming to have a bad back (he knew that back problems are difficult to diagnose and had managed to get a doctor's certificate to support this), and b) would quite often stay up all night and go to work in order to sleep in the computer room, which he had cleverly rigged up to provide him with an early warning system. He'd be quite open about his outrageous skiving to colleagues he knew well. He managed to get away with it for three years until he realized he was deeply bored, found a different job and gave up slacking for good.

Sarah, on the other hand, was far more irritating. Her days were spent slacking in the office in the various different ways described on page 99, but mainly by roaming the office talking to people – whether they liked it or not. She very rarely did any work, and when she did it was at a snail's pace during moments snatched between long sessions of inactivity. She had managed to achieve and maintain this situation by claiming to have far too much work to do, and actually freelanced out the majority of her work. She got away with it partly because she was the only person in the office who did her particular job (as contracts manager), and partly because everyone else in the office was too nice to shop her.

other signs of stress such as hand-wringing and hair-pulling and weeping.

The Crisis Monkey will definitely not keep the crisis to themselves, and will try to enlist the help of anyone who does a similar job, works in the same department or, failing that, anyone who looks vaguely sympathetic. They will usually be hopelessly disorganized, adding to the potential for genuine crises.

The Crisis Monkey might also be a Loon, a Late Worker or a Complainer.

The Champion Slacker

Everyone who works in an office is a slacker for part of the time, but Champion Slackers are the idlers who manage to spend more time slacking than working. They can be subdivided into two types: those who admit their appalling behaviour to colleagues and don't care too much if they get sacked (it's difficult not to admire, or at least be amused by, this type of slacker); and those who pretend to work hard, not realizing that their idleness is plain to all and deeply irritating to those who have to deal with the effects of their feckless behaviour.

The Management-Speaker

There will probably be lots of people in your office who are regular users of management-speak. Thrusters, Tigers and

> *I suspect guys who say, 'I just send out for a sandwich for lunch,' as lazy men trying to impress me.*
> **Jimmy Cannon**

Whoopers are all very likely to be impressed by it, as well as the whole of the Marketing and Sales department. The official title of Management-Speaker should go to whoever uses it the most. This might be very difficult to judge. To help you, turn the page for a comprehensive Dictionary of Management-Speak.

A Dictionary of Management-Speak

Managers hardly ever do anything clever, and many of them hardly ever do anything at all. It's important that they disguise this as much as possible by making it sound as though their work is complicated and important. This is achieved via management-speak.

In fact, management-speak serves several different purposes: first of all, every field has its technical terms, and managers don't see why theirs should be any different. But, whereas technical language is designed to save time and provide clarity, management-speak wastes as much time as possible and confuses everybody. Of course, this can come in very handy if you need to talk euphemistically about something unpalatable, like 'smartsizing' or 'sunsetting'.

Using management-speak also helps to set management apart from the rank and file, who hopefully won't understand most of it. Managers hope that when they say things like 'Let's put some wood behind the arrow!' people will be impressed. It also helps to disguise ignorance – you could say that you're 'concentrating on improving business development and qualitizing product' in answer to almost any question without having to know anything at all.

Many management-speakers feel that they are suggesting an air of transatlantic sophistication by using US terms –

baseball terminology seems to be a particular favourite – but this is hopelessly misjudged. This type of language only suggests an air of a British corporate moron trying to sound like an American corporate moron and failing.

Because managers don't like to admit it if they don't understand what particular management-speak words and phrases mean, some management-speak is used to mean different things, and sometimes a particular company adopts a meaning unilaterally. Often, management-speakers themselves only have a hazy idea of what a word or phrase they are using actually means. For this reason, definitions are sometimes difficult to pin down exactly.

Some words included in the dictionary, such as 'arsemosis', aren't necessarily used by management-speakers but can be used to describe them. Also, some of the jargon included is from particular industries – the Stock Exchange, for example – so it's not used in most offices. But phrases like 'dead cat bounce' are too irresistible to leave out. Perhaps you could try using some jargon from other industries to confuse the management-speakers in your office. In time it may get taken up, though no one will be quite sure what it means.

In fact, instead of playing Bullshit Bingo in meetings, perhaps you and your like-minded colleagues could score points for every management-speak word you make up yourself and successfully introduce into the company lexicon. Management-speak is full of ordinary nouns turned into ridiculous verbs and vice versa (such as 'learning' as a noun, or 'action' as a verb), and words such as 'qualitize' that sound suspiciously like Bushisms. Fabricate a few of these and throw them into the conversation – 'strategemize' or the noun 'oppose', for example.

> *The highest reward for a person's toil is not what they get for it, but what they become by it.*
>
> **John Ruskin**

The Dictionary

12-o'clock flasher (phrase): an IT term for someone who is technologically challenged: the idea is that all the electrical equipment in his or her home constantly flashes 12:00 because the technophobe hasn't been able to set it.

24/7 (phrase): this has become a management-speak favourite: 'I want to see us working on this growth strategy 24/7'. Even worse is its successor, '24/7/365'.

360-degree view (phrase): management-speakers prefer this to 'all-round view' or similar phrases, maybe because it has numbers in it.

800-lb gorilla (phrase): dominant company or person – sometimes a fairly accurate physical description. For example, 'Who's the 800-lb gorilla at Acme?' Also **big white chief**.

30,000-foot level (phrase): see **big picture**.

action (verb): qualifies as management-speak only when used as a verb, for example: 'I'll action that immediately.' Note also the adjective '**actionable**': 'Are there any actionable items on that list?'

> *As you know, nothing worth knowing can be explained with regular words.*
>
> **Scott Adams, *Dilbert and the Way of the Weasel***

action-item (noun): something **actionable**, or in need of being **actioned**.

adversarial shopper (noun): bargain hunter – note the interesting choice of adjective.

aha! (noun): revelation or surprise – and it's certainly surprising that anyone should feel able to use this word in all seriousness. For example, 'There were several **aha!**s in that presentation.' Also **showstopper.**

all over the map (phrase): confused. For example, 'Brian's presentation was all over the map. He totally **blew his buffer**.'

alpha geek (noun): most technically knowledgeable employee. Note that IT staff will want to kill anyone they hear using this phrase.

analysis paralysis (noun): research instead of action. Management-speakers will expect you to be impressed by the rhyme.

around the horn (phrase): giving everyone the chance to take part in a discussion. Users of this phrase might know that it was originally a baseball term, in which case they will feel extra smug about using it.

> *Work to survive, survive by consuming, survive to consume: the hellish cycle is complete.*
>
> **Raoul Vaneigen**

arrow shooter (noun): it's always best to use a pompous image like this one instead of using ordinary words like visionary or ideas person.

arrows to fire (noun): points to make in support of an argument. See above.

arsemosis (noun): process of becoming successful via brown-nosing.

asap (verb): this becomes particularly excruciating when used as a verb and pronounced 'assap'. For example, 'I'll asap that **action-item**.'

automagic (noun): particularly annoying way of saying 'technology', often used by managers seeking to suck up to the IT department (who will only despise them for it).

B2B (noun or adjective): business that sells to other businesses – but much more important-sounding.

B2C (noun or adjective): business that sells to customers – see above.

B2D (noun or adjective): business that sels to a distributor – see above.

B2G (noun or adjective): business that sells to the government – see above.

bait and switch (phrase): a sales term meaning to offer something unavailable as 'bait', then, once the customer is interested, replace it with something inferior. People who use management-speak will be impressed by this manoeuvre.

bake (verb): Saying you're going to 'bake a feature into something' sounds so much more impressive than just including it.

ballpark (verb): to estimate (see **ballpark figure**).

ballpark figure (noun): rough figure. Conjuring up the heady world of (preferably US) sport always appeals to a management-speaker.

banana problem (noun) a problem with a simple solution. The idea is that it's so simple a monkey could work it out: monkeys like bananas … er … it all makes sense if you're in management.

bandaid (noun and verb): a temporary solution. The word has the obvious advantage of being American. Note that it can be used as a verb for management-speak bonus points:

'Can the programmers bandaid that software?' See also **quick and dirty fix**.

bandwidth (noun): capacity, but with the added bonus of sounding vaguely technical. For example, 'Do we have the bandwidth to increase our customer base?'

beat the Street (verb): used about a company, meaning to perform better than the Stock Exchange (Wall Street) predicted. Impressed?

benchmark (noun and verb): at its most annoying when used as a verb, meaning to set something as a standard. For example, 'Let's benchmark this product for **PVM**.'

best in breed (adjective): the highest quality: 'We want to stand out as best in breed: let's get to work on our **channel strategy**!'

best practice: highest industry standard. For example, 'We've configured this **box** according to best practice.'

betamaxed (adjective): more impressive and potentially confusing than saying something has been superseded and rendered out-of-date. Also **dead technology**.

big bang (verb and noun): launch. Particularly annoying when used as a verb: 'We'll big bang this product in April.'

> *It was not the man's brain that was speaking, it was his larynx. The stuff that was coming out of him consisted of words, but it was not speech in the true sense: it was a noise uttered in unconsciousness, like the quacking of a duck.*
> George Orwell, *Nineteen Eighty-Four*

big picture (noun): an old favourite of management-speakers, meaning the wider view. Seeing the big picture is a good thing. It might even be might be 'viewed from **30,000 feet**'. See also **helicopter view**.

big wheel (noun): important person. For example, 'I know Smithers is a big wheel at ABC, but who's the **800-lb gorilla**?'

big white chief (noun): see **800-lb gorilla**.

bile factor (noun): the amount of hatred harboured by employees towards the company they work for.

blamestorm (noun and verb): meeting convened to assess a failed project and assign blame. If there's been a **learning experience**, everyone involved will be anticipating a blamestorm.

bleeding edge (adjective): usually applied to technology which is not yet ready to be used. The idea is that it's so cutting-edge you could cut yourself on it – note that management-speakers will expect you to be amused and/or impressed by this term, at least for the first fifty or so times they use it.

blowing your buffer (phrase): if you lose your train of thought in a meeting or presentation you've blown your buffer ... and perhaps your chances of promotion too.

> *Work saves us from three great evils: boredom, vice and need.*
> **Voltaire**

bluesky (verb): to think imaginatively and creatively – management-speakers do a lot of this. It's also possible to have 'bluesky ideas'. See also **think outside the box**.

body slam (noun): a lucrative sale. You're supposed to be imagining an ice-hockey player smashing into an opponent. Sigh.

boil the ocean dry (phrase): to cover every possible option. For example, 'We've already boiled the ocean – we can't make this any more cost-effective.'

bottom fishing (verb): to buy stock that is going down or has already gone down in value drastically. Why not impress and/or confuse your manager by dropping this into the conversation?

bottom line (noun): another old management-speak favourite meaning 'the fundamental or deciding factor'. For example, 'The bottom line is that we need to **embrace change** to achieve optimal **brand management** and meet our **stretch targets**.'

bounce [usually an idea] off someone (phrase): If you'd like someone's reaction to something new, why not suggest that you 'bounce an idea' off them? The two of you could even 'bounce a few ideas around'. Then you could take the idea to a meeting, and **run it up the flagpole and see if anyone salutes**.

box (noun): IT term for server. If management-speakers have heard the word they'll use it as often as possible, desperately hoping for the chance to explain it to someone else and thereby appear technically knowledgeable.

brain dump (noun and verb): ludicrous way of saying providing information, for example for a job handover. Probably most ridiculous as a verb: 'You'll need to brain dump on that project so that I can **hit the ground running**.' Also sometimes used (erroneously) as a synonym for brainstorm. Also **data dump**.

braggables (noun): products to, er, brag about.

brand management (noun): a whole pseudo-science – it sounds like nonsense and no doubt it is.

breadcrumb level (noun): detailed, or **granular** – the opposite of the **big picture**.

broad-gauged (adjective): broad-minded, prepared to **think outside the box**.

build a better mousetrap (phrase): be inventive or clever, no doubt using **joined-up thinking** and perhaps **blueskying**.

bury the bodies (verb): hide the evidence of an error. For example, 'Well, that was a **learning experience**. Now we need to bury the bodies before the **big wheels** find out.'

buy-in (noun and verb): agreement or approval. Note that you can get someone's buy-in, or someone can buy into something.

byte-bonding (verb): technical people getting to know one another better by talking about technology, rather than more usual social interaction. Management-speakers think they are highly socially skilled and like to draw attention to it with snide remarks about technical staff.

cascade (verb): if you imagine the company hierarchy forming a human pyramid with the CEO at the top balancing on the shoulders of two members of senior management, everyone holding a champagne glass, then a giant bottle of champagne being poured into the first glass, overflowing and filling the glasses on the next layer down, and so on – this is what you're supposed to envisage, except with information instead of champagne.

cash cow (noun): something extremely profitable. For example, 'Our biggest cash cow is having a **halo effect** on some of our less **optimal** products.'

catch a falling knife (phrase): a Stock Market phrase meaning to buy stock as it goes down in value, hoping that it will shortly go up again, but find that it continues to go down.

chainsaw consultant (noun): consultant brought in to **downsize**, **rightsize** or **smartsize**.

challenge (noun): problem.

change management (noun): change is always a good thing (see **embracing change**), but it does need very careful management.

channel (noun): market, but slightly more technical-sounding. Marketing departments will have 'channel strategies' and 'channel managers'.

chips and salsa (noun): hardware and software. As with **box**, **tin**, **malware**, etc., management-speakers will take enormous pleasure in explaining this if someone doesn't know what they mean.

circle back (verb): management-speakers often suggest that we 'circle back for a moment' – they might mean going back to the beginning, or maybe revisiting a particular point. Who knows?

circling the drain (phrase): can be used about an employee who is about to be fired (see also **departure lounge**), or a project that's about to be cancelled.

client-centric (adjective): see **customer-focused**.

clockless worker (noun): an employee who is willing to work any time and any number of hours. Once they've burnt themselves out through overwork, management will make sure they're **rifted**.

coach (noun): boss (note the sporting reference). Likely to be used in a **flat management structure**.

cobwebsite (noun): website that hasn't been updated for a long time. (Another instance of what passes for management humour.)

cockroach problem (noun): a major problem. The opposite of a **banana problem**.

competency (noun): a Human Resources word for skill or requirement. See also **proficiency**.

conference (verb): in management-speak, used as a verb in place of 'have a meeting': 'We should conference on our **channel strategy**.'

connect the dots (phrase): to put together the implications. For example, 'If you connect the dots you'll see that the project is **circling the drain**.' This phrase sounds impressive and allows for possible confusion, both very good things.

> *Process and Procedure are the last hiding place of people without the wit and wisdom to do their job properly.*
> **Anonymous**

consumer-driven (adjective): see **customer-focused**.

continuous improvement (phrase): obviously this is a good thing, but management-speakers often say they are looking to achieve it as though they'd just thought of a brilliant new idea.

core (adjective): a word favoured by management-speakers. It usually means 'essential', and always refers to something positive, such as 'core **competencies/proficiencies**', which are either essential skills or strong points, depending on the context: for example, 'innovation is one of this company's core proficiencies', or, 'you need to be able to juggle for this role – it's a core proficiency'.

cost management (noun): another area that needs careful management, often resulting in **revectoring**, **downsizing**, **rightsizing** or **smartsizing**.

crack troops (noun): the workforce. Often used in pep talks by the CEO or equivalent, especially if announcing bad news.

CRM (acronym): Customer Relationship Management. Management-speakers will try to catch you out with acronyms.

customer-focused (adjective): see **client-centric**.

CYA (acronym): Cover Your Arse (or Ass, in the original).

data dump (verb): see **brain dump**.

dead cat bounce (phrase): the phenomenon of stock going up in price having made a sudden fall, because people have seen it fall and are rushing to buy.

dead technology (noun): see **betamaxed**.

decommission (verb): to sack.

decruit (verb): to sack.

deep dive (verb): to go into a lot of detail. For example, 'We can deep dive on this issue **offline**.'

dehire (verb): to sack.

deinstall (verb): to sack.

delayer (verb): to strip away levels of management – often thereby **empowering** the workforce.

deliverable (noun): acceptable as an adjective, deliverable becomes management-speak when used as a noun – for example, 'Give me a list of deliverables for next Spring's **big bang**'.

departure lounge (noun): staff who are 'in the departure lounge' are about to be (or likely to be) sacked or made redundant.

dial it back (phrase): another confusing phrase, which probably means 'review something', or possibly 'go back to the beginning', but no one is quite sure.

dip our toes in the water (phrase): to try something (a business plan or a partnership, for example) without being committed to it. You will have to try not to imagine senior management barefoot with their trousers rolled up.

disconnect (noun): another ridiculous nouning, which means a bad business relationship or misunderstanding. For example, there might be a disconnect between finance and marketing, either on a specific issue or as an ongoing situation.

disintermediation (noun): cutting out the middle man, using an unnecesarily long word that you hope will make you sound clever. See also **reintermediation**.

dog and pony show (noun): strange term for a big corporate presentation conducted by company **big wheels**. It must make sense to senior management.

dogfood (verb): to test a new company product in-house. For example, 'We should dogfood that software before it ships.'

download (noun): yet another example of a verb being made into a very annoying noun, which in this case means information. For example, 'I'll give you the download on that project after the meeting.'

downside risk (phrase): opposite of **upside potential**.

drill down (verb): to analyse something in more detail. Management-speakers will often 'drill down into the data' or **deep dive**.

drink from a fire hydrant (phrase): try to extract a small and specific piece of information from a very large database. For example, 'I made the mistake of asking Bill from IT to explain the downtime. It was like drinking from a fire hydrant.'

drink the Kool-aid (verb): to be enthusiatic about a project/business plan, or generally toe the company line: 'If you want to hang on to your job at this company you have to **drink the Kool-aid**.' See also **pour the Kool-aid**.

driving ducks to a poor pond (phrase): not making enough money to avoid going bust.

drool-proof (adjective): idiot-proof. Particularly used by IT, who see all non-technical people as drooling morons.

drop-dead date (noun): extra important deadline. Everything is important to management-speakers, so they need phrases that mean 'even more important than usual' like this one.

drop paper (verb): to contract or conclude a deal, often in writing. For example, 'Have we dropped paper yet? Friday's the **drop-dead date**.'

drop the ball (verb): to mess up. For example, 'Marketing dropped the ball and we lost the account. Now two of them are in the **departure lounge**.'

drop your pants (verb): especially disturbing phrase meaning to lower-price to get a sale. For example, the sales director might say, 'We'll have to drop our pants by 30K to make this deal.' You have to try not to call an image to mind.

ducks in a row (phrase): management-speakers get their ducks in a row instead of simply 'preparing'.

duck soup (adjective): simple. Management-speakers will

enjoy the fact that no one knows what they're talking about for the first few times they use this phrase.

eat our own dogfood (phrase): see **dogfood**.

echo bubble (noun): a sharp rise in stock following a sharp fall (a bit like a **dead cat bounce**).

Elvis year (noun): the period in which something was at its most popular: for example, the Rubik's Cube's Elvis year was 1982.

embrace (verb): management-speakers are fond of embracing things, particularly change. For example, 'We are seeking **continuous improvement** on a **go forward basis**, therefore we need to embrace change.'

embrace and extend (phrase): to copy another company's product and add a few extra features. (Note the euphemistic use of 'embrace'.)

empower (verb): management-speakers love this word. You might find them empowering their customers with greater choice, or empowering their staff with more responsibility

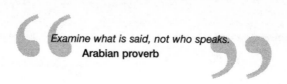

Examine what is said, not who speaks.
Arabian proverb

(although usually the staff aren't given any extra authority or money).

enabler (noun): another favoured word, which is vague but also sounds good. Management will all see themselves as enablers, of course.

enhance (verb): management-speakers often favour this word over 'improve' or 'add to'. They might enhance their client base, sales, customer service, brand management or product – ideally on a **go forward basis**.

envisioneering (verb): see **imagineering**.

event horizon (noun): the point of no return. In physics, an event horizon is the edge of a black hole, so management-speakers think it sounds extra clever. Also **tipping point**.

face time (noun): personal meeting: 'Let's all try to achieve more face time with our clients.'

fair-haired children (noun): young high-flyers (or **HI-POTs**) whom the company wants to nurture – usually tossers of the highest order.

fall down the cracks (phrase): to get lost, often used as a blame-evasion phrase.

feature creep (noun): see **scope creep**.

feedback (noun): management-speakers are extremely keen on feedback, unless it's the negative kind or about them.

file 13 (noun): the bin. Management-speakers don't have a sense of humour, so they use language like this thinking it compensates.

finger in the air (phrase): give a rough estimate (or **ball-park**). For example, 'Give me a finger in the air on total revenue based on achieving that **stretch target**.'

flag up (verb): the preferred management-speak way of saying 'point out'.

flat management structure (noun): a management structure that has been **delayered**. As mentioned earlier, the boss will probably wear a lot of corduroy and think he's creative and very cool.

flight risk (noun): employees are seen as a flight risk if they are suspected of being about to leave. This is only a problem if they are **fair-haired children**.

> *Prose consists less and less of WORDS chosen for the sake of their meaning, and more and more of PHRASES tacked together like the sections of a prefabricated hen-house.*
> **George Orwell**

foot soldiers (noun): see **headcount**.

frictionless (adjective): smooth (!).

from soup to nuts (phrase): from start to finish (perplexingly).

front-burner (noun and verb): prioritize. Note that you can 'put something on the front-burner' but you can also (and more toe-curlingly) 'front-burner something'.

full pipeline (phrase): busy. Managers' pipelines are almost always full.

future-proof (adjective): unlikely to date quickly, particuarly used of technology by management-speakers who don't know what they're talking about.

game plan (noun): management-speak for strategy (note the sporting reference): 'If we're going to **run with this monkey**, we need a watertight game plan.'

gap analysis (noun): used by management in an attempt to make what they do seem more difficult than it really is.

get in at the ground floor (phrase): be in on a project or company at the start. For example, 'This project is **going gang busters** so it was excellent strategy to get in at the ground floor.'

get into bed with (phrase): particularly disturbing phrase meaning working closely with a colleague or company, possibly going into a partnership. For example, 'You'll need to get into bed with Simpson on this one.'

get lost in the noise (verb): to be overlooked, or **fall down the cracks**.

gigadeal (noun): very large deal – even larger than a **megadeal**. Again, management-speakers will feel smug about using terminology related to IT.

go figure (phrase): management-speakers would far rather use this phrase than a more British one such as 'work *that* one out' because it's from the US and therefore naturally more corporate.

goal-focused (adjective): management-speakers are very goal-focused (or goal-directed), and will tell you about it a lot.

going forward (phrase): into the future. For example, 'We're utilizing this policy going forward'. Or you might find that something is happening 'on a going forward basis' or, even worse, 'on a go forward basis'.

going gang-busters (phrase): going exceptionally well, but described in an exceptionally annoying way.

going postal (phrase): going bonkers, possibly violently so. Refers to various cases of US postal workers going mad with shotguns – management-speakers will no doubt be pleased with the US connection and it might also appeal to their non-sense of humour.

goldbrick (noun): an office worker who spends his or her time trying to look valuable, rather than actually doing anything of any value.

golden handcuffs (noun): huge salary paid to someone the company doesn't want to leave.

golden parachute (noun): huge severance money paid to senior managers.

governance (noun): management-speakers often use this instead of 'management', thinking it sounds cleverer.

grab the easy meat (verb): to take the easily available gains, rather like **picking the low-hanging fruit.**

granular (adjective): detailed. Management-speakers will like to talk about **granularity** a lot, too. For example, 'Can we get greater granularity on those figures? We need to **deep dive** on this one.'

groin pull (noun): an overly agreessive or macho stance that results in alienating colleagues or customers. Ugh.

guesstimate (noun and verb): management-speakers greatly prefer this over 'estimate', even though there's no difference in meaning.

halo effect (noun): the beneficial effect a best-selling product can have on others in the company's range. 'We've achieved excellent sales with this product: it could have a halo effect on our other **merch**.'

hardball: see **play hardball**.

hard stop (noun): the time at which a meeting (for example) has to end, used by people who think they are more important than anyone else: 'I have a hard stop at four, will this take any longer than an hour?'

headcount (noun): the company's rank-and-file employees. Also **foot soldiers** (which is less pejorative).

heads-up (noun): warning. For example, 'I'm giving you a heads-up on some **challenges** in this project.'

helicopter view (noun): if you're taking a helicopter view you can be sure you are seeing the **big picture**. Managers need to take a helicopter view as often as possible, while the **headcount** gets on with the actual work.

high-dome (noun): egghead: 'Let's get the high-domes to come up with some **automagic**.'

HI-POTs (noun): employees considered to have HIgh career POTential. They will no doubt be **fair-haired children**.

hit the ground running (phrase): management-speakers don't like to waste any time, so it's important that when they're passed a project they (or preferably somebody else) are **up to speed** and can carry on with it straight away.

ho-hum product (noun): an everyday product, for example, safety-pins, where it's difficult to tell the difference between brands: 'We should be totally **profit-driven** with this – it's a ho-hum product.'

hot button (noun): an important and/or emotionally charged issue: 'Don't mention the **smartsizing** – it's a hot button issue right now.'

human capital (noun): one step on from the term 'human resources', and even more offensive.

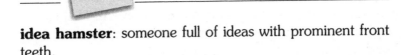

Life grants nothing to us mortals without hard work.
Horace

idea hamster: someone full of ideas with prominent front teeth.

imagineering (verb): a very clever combination of two separate words: 'imagining' and 'engineering' (do you see how that works?). Put the two together and you get a word which is supposed to convey the idea of putting visions into practice, but in fact just really gets on everyone's nerves. Also **envisioneering** (if anything even worse).

impact (verb): only qualifies as management-speak when used as a verb. For example, 'How is the new policy impacting on growth in that **channel**?'

I'm loving/lovin' it (phrase): middle-aged management-speakers might say this in meetings thinking they sound hip. How tragically wrong they are.

incent (verb): managers might 'incent' staff instead of offering them an incentive.

incentivize (verb): even more ridiculous way of saying **incent**.

inchpebble (noun): small milestone. Another example of management humour (see also **file 13**, **mural dyslexia**, etc).

Indian initiative (noun): an idea which came from the **foot soldiers**.

integrated solution (phrase): a solution in which various different aspects work together. In other words, a solution.

interface (verb): this perfectly acceptable word becomes corporate nonsense when turned into a verb and used to mean 'meet'. For example, 'Let's interface Tuesday!'

in the zone (phrase): concentrating and working especially productively – management-speakers find that they're in the zone a lot.

issue (noun): problem. Also **challenge** or **opportunity**.

joined-up thinking (phrase): thinking about an issue or problem in an intelligent way. In other words, being clever. Again, management-speakers do a lot of this. For example, 'We used joined-up thinking and **enhanced** our **game plan** to achieve **continuous improvement**.'

join the dots (verb): see **connect the dots**.

jump on the grenade (verb): to try to limit damage only to end up in a much worse position. For example, 'We lost that feature because costs were way too high – now all the orders are cancelled. Looks like we jumped on the grenade.'

jury-proof (adjective): able stand up under scrutiny. For example, 'It looks good from where I'm standing, but is it jury-proof?'

keep [someone] in the loop (phrase): to keep someone informed, but phrased much more annoyingly.

key (adjective): important. Like **core**, this word is used a lot in management-speak: you might have key customers, key drivers and key managers, for example.

kicking the tyres (phrase): testing something out, usually before buying it. For example, 'The client wants to kick the tyres – he's asked for a free trial.'

knock something out of the park (phrase): to exceed expectations – very much like a game of baseball. Management-speakers will particularly like the US sport reference. Also **knock the cover off the ball**.

knowledge capital (noun): a resource held by the **human capital**.

L

learning (noun): a particularly farcical nouning of an ordinary verb. Used as in, 'We gained considerable learning from that **challenge**.'

learning experience (noun): complete disaster.

level set (verb): to make sure everyone is fully informed, or **up to speed**, often so that people are able to **hit the ground running**.

leverage (verb): this common management-speak verb almost always simply means 'use'. For example, 'We need to leverage our resources in order to maximise revenue.'

leverageable (adjective): usable.

lie down with lions (phrase): to make a business deal with ruthless individuals or a company, while making it sound a lot scarier.

line up the ducks (phrase): see **ducks in a row**.

long pole (noun): something or someone holding up a project (from long pole in the tent – geddit?).

loop, the (noun): see **keep in the loop** and **out of the loop**.

lose the bubble (verb): lose concentration, possibly resulting in **blowing your buffer**.

low-hanging fruit (noun): easy gains (or **wins**). For example, 'Our **key** customers will all be interested in the new product – speak to them first and pick the low-hanging fruit before you move on to other customers.'

malware (noun): malicious software. Another word that management-speakers enjoy using because it makes them sound technically knowledgeable.

manage expectations (verb): everything needs managing, including expectations. Usually this means making sure people aren't disappointed, but put like this it sounds a lot more involved.

If oratory is a lost art, let's leave it that way.
Anonymous

management by exception (phrase): only getting involved when there's a problem – and usually doing very little as a result.

market pathfinder (noun): a person who's discovered a way of accessing a new market. For example, if you discovered you could sell your company's excess stock of cheese-and-onion crisps to the building industry as roof insulation, you'd be a market pathfinder.

megadeal (noun): large deal, though not quite so big as a **gigadeal**.

merch (noun): short for merchandise and used by management-speakers in a hurry (presumably).

methodology (noun): a real word rendered meaningless by people who don't know how to use it, beloved of management-speakers.

me-too product (noun): product that copies another one already on the market. This phrase has the benefit of being euphemistic and will be less familiar than 'copy'.

metric (noun): management-speakers use this technical word to mean a measurement of success, hoping it sounds somehow scientific. For example, 'These metrics serve to quantify our goal of continuous improvement.'

mindshare (noun and verb): sharing information. Only the most flagrant management-speakers can bring themselves to use this ridiculous word.

mission-critical (adjective): pompous way of saying 'essential for success'.

monkey see, monkey do (phrase): used about someone who doesn't have a clue why they're doing something, but blindly copies procedure. A bit like following the Mirror, Signal, Manoeuvre procedure but not taking any notice of what's actually *in* the mirror.

moon the giant (phrase): insult or disparage a powerful business rival. For example, 'We need to keep a low profile if we're to poach some of Acme's business, so be careful not to moon the giant.'

more bang for your buck (phrase): the best result for the least amount of effort. The use of this phrase is limited to the more shameless management-speakers.

mural dyslexia (noun): someone with this condition 'can't see the writing on the wall'. Another example of what passes for management humour (see also **file 13**, **inchpebble**, etc.).

my world (phrase): job, or area of expertise. See also **not in my world**.

new world (noun): the company after a restructure. For example, 'In the new world, ours will be a more **client-centric** environment.'

no-brainer (noun): something that is so easy or obvious it doesn't need thinking about. For example, 'This strategy increases revenue and cuts back on staff: it's a no-brainer, implement it at once.' Also **zero-sum**.

no guts no glory (phrase): 'who dares wins' for management.

not in my world (phrase): outside my area. For example, 'I don't deal with the customers directly, that's not in my world.' Management-speakers might discover that their world gets bigger, too. (If it gets smaller they tend to keep quiet about it.)

oar in the water (phrase): if someone has their oar in the water they are working as a **team player**. If they don't, they're not pulling their weight and might well already be in the **departure lounge**.

offline (adjective): see **talk offline**.

on-message (adjective): someone who is on-message is a mouthpiece for company policy – not only **drinking the Kool-Aid** but spouting it too. Management-speakers ensure they are on-message at all times.

on the same page (phrase): sharing the same objectives and information: 'We need to make sure we're on the same page before we **run with this monkey**.' Also **singing from the same hymn sheet**.

open the kimono (phrase): to disclose privileged information. This conjures a particularly unpleasant image of senior management.

operating in a silo (phrase): if you're doing this you're not being a good team player, which is one of management's deadly sins. Note that it's also possible to '**silo**' information, i.e. keep it to yourself.

opportunity (noun): problem. Also **challenge** and **issue**.

out of the loop (phrase): uninformed. Often this is used as an excuse: if you'd been in the loop you would have been told what was going on, and could have been **proactive**, but someone failed to inform you.

> *Women do not win formula one races, because they simply are not strong enough to resist the G-forces. In the boardroom, it is different. I believe women are better able to marshal their thoughts than men and because they are less egotistical they make fewer assumptions.*
> **Henry Ford**

outplace (verb): to sack.

outside the box (phrase): see **thinking outside the box.**

outside the square (phrase): see **thinking outside the box.**

over the line (phrase): management-speak for 'over the top'. For example, 'Marketing are worried that their policy of selling directly to children in school playgrounds might be over the line.'

own (verb): to be responsible for, but supposedly without the negative connotations. Management is fond of delegating ownership.

parachute someone in (verb): to bring in someone from outside the company to do a particular job. This phrase makes it sound a bit like being part of the Resistance or, maybe preferable to management-speakers, Rambo.

paradigm (noun): shared set of beliefs or way of working. 'Paradigm' is a big favourite with management-speakers, who often view problems as being created by an outdated paradigm. The solution is a **paradigm shift**.

paradigm shift (phrase): a change in the company's or the market's belief system: 'We've effected a paradigm shift which is the major cause of increased profits and efficiency.'

parking lot (verb): to postpone. For example, 'We'll have to parking lot that **action-item** until we have more **feedback**.'

pass the baton (verb): to hand over (note the sporting reference): 'Make sure you **data dump** before you pass the baton to Sales.'

pat the dog (phrase): incredibly patronizing way of saying 'praise': 'My assistant did most of the work on that deal, so I made sure I patted the dog.'

payroll orphans (noun): employees who have been sacked or made redundant.

peel the onion (phrase): to **delayer** something (often a problem) until you've got to the root of it: 'Let's peel the onion here and find out why achieving these goals is becoming a **challenge**.'

permalancer (noun): permanent freelancer who might spend years at a company without receiving any benefits whatsoever.

pick the low-hanging fruit (verb): see **low-hanging fruit** and **grab the easy meat**.

pitch in a lift (phrase): quick outline or debrief: 'I have a **hard stop** in five minutes: give me a pitch in a lift.' But most managers would rather say things the long and confusing way.

play hardball (verb): to deal ruthlessly with individuals or other companies. Management-speakers will definitely expect you to be impressed if they're about to play hardball.

pound the table (verb): to enthuse: 'The management team needs to pound the table and **ramp up** this project.'

pour the Kool-Aid (verb): to be in charge, dictating policies etc. Subordinates should **drink the Kool-Aid**. (Kool-Aid is a US brand of soft drink – why it's been chosen as a symbol of corporate nonsense is a mystery.)

press the flesh (verb): shake hands, or meet in person, but described in the most annoying way possible.

proactive (adjective): the opposite of reactive. For example, 'This software will proactively scan the network and let you know about problems before they happen.'

proficiency (noun): Human Resources word for skill. See also **competency**.

profit-driven (adjective): focused on hard cash and indifferent to quality, customers or anything else.

pull-aside (noun): an informal, unplanned meeting. For example, 'I initiated a beneficial pull-aside at the trade fair with the CEO of Acme.'

pull down the shade (phrase): get down to business: 'Let's pull down the shade and focus on our growth strategy.'

pull up the manhole covers and look down the drains (phrase): examine thoroughly.

push back (verb): to disagree with or question something. For example, 'Push back on that point and see if you can get him to agree to our terms.'

push the envelope (phrase): to stretch limitations or parameters. Management-speakers who like to **bluesky** and **think outside the box** will often push the envelope too.

put skin in the game (phrase): invest money in something: 'Are we confident enough about the prototype to put some skin in the game?'

put some pants on something (phrase): to fill in all the details of an idea, accompanied by an amusing image.

put some wood behind the arrow (phrase): to put marketing, money or other resources behind a product or company. In some cases, *all* of the wood is put behind *one* arrow, but this is usually ill-advised.

put to bed (verb): finish.

put your foot on the ball and look up (phrase): stop what you're doing and look at the **bigger picture**.

PVM (noun): Perceived Value for Money. Management speakers often use acronyms hoping to confuse you.

qualitize (verb): to add quality. This could almost be a Bushism.

quick and dirty fix/solution (phrase): *see* **bandaid**.

raise a red flag (phrase): give a warning: 'I hate to raise a red flag, but there are some potential **challenges** in dealing with this **channel**.'

raise the bar (phrase): set higher targets. You are supposed to be envisioning an athlete clearing a high jump, which may be difficult when you are looking at a shiny-suited middle-manager.

ramp up (verb): to increase investment or enthusiasm: 'Jim's going to ramp up the new product with **key** clients.'

reach out (verb): management-speakers use this to give an impression of compassion and selflessness, instead of just saying they're giving someone a hand or passing on some information.

reality check (noun and verb): step back and look at something objectively. For maximum cringe-making effect it can be shorted to RC. For example, 'I'd been **pounding the table** about this project for weeks when I realized it was time for an RC.'

RC (noun and verb): see **reality check**.

reintermediation (noun): putting back the middle man, using an unnecesarily long word that you hope will make you sound clever. See also **disintermediation**.

reinventing the wheel (phrase): unwittingly producing something that's already been done: 'The programmer was working on that software for six months but ended up reinventing the wheel.'

---

results-driven (adjective): see **profit-driven** (since profit is usually the main 'result' on manager's mind).

revector (verb): to change the business plan, often resulting in **downsizing**, **rightsizing** or **smartsizing**.

rifted (adjective): sacked (from Reduction In Force).

rightsize (verb): euphemism for **downsize**, which is itself a euphemism for random sackings.

road builders (noun): practical employees who pave the way for the **arrow shooters'** ideas to be put into practice.

rocket science (noun): management-speakers will constantly remind you that what they're talking about 'isn't rocket science', implying that if anyone's finding it difficult, they can't be as bright as the management-speaker.

roll up (verb): compile. For example, 'I'll roll up these figures for the next meeting.' Roll up is probably used because it sounds less straightforward and might make people think something clever is going on.

ruggedize (verb): to make a delicate product suitable for use in the field. For example, 'Our product falls apart every time someone uses it: perhaps we need to ruggedize.'

run something up the flagpole and see if anyone

salutes (phrase): try something out and gauge reaction to it. This phrase is often accompanied by a little laugh, as if it were being used ironically: it's not, management-speakers don't understand irony. Also **throw something at the wall and see if it sticks**.

run with this monkey [let's] (phrase): management speakers sometimes use this expression at the start of a new project they're excited about. No one knows why.

scope creep (noun): increase in the goals or expectations of a project. For example, 'Project X has a terrible case of scope creep the nearer it gets to the **drop dead date**.' Also **feature creep**.

see the big picture (phrase): see **big picture**.

see what's coming down the pike (phrase): be aware of what's likely to happen (pike = turnpike) – not having **mural dyslexia**.

serial entrepeneur (noun): someone who has started several new businesses and is therefore incredibly impressive to management-speakers.

sharpen your saw (phrase): to become more effective at your job, often through training. For example, 'That time-management training course has really sharpened my saw.'

showstopper (noun): see **aha!**

shuffle the deckchairs (phrase): rearrange without doing anything. (The phrase comes from 'shuffling the deckchairs on the *Titanic*'.) For example, 'Marketing are doing more research because the product's **tanking**, but really they're just shuffling the deckchairs.'

silo (verb): see **operating in a silo**.

singing from the same hymn sheet (phrase): another old favourite, meaning **on the same page**.

skill set (noun): managers like to refer to skill sets because they sound more wide-ranging and also more vague than 'qualifications'.

skin in the game (phrase): see **put skin in the game**.

slam dunk (noun): an easy sale/gain – a basketball phrase, so management-speakers will no doubt feel particularly smug about using it.

smartsize (verb): see **rightsize**.

SME (noun): Subject Matter Expert. Pronounced 'smee'. Note the management-speak tactics of using an acronym as a bamboozling tool, and also the complete redundancy of two of the three words.

soft copy (noun): electronic document. A term guaranteed to annoy anyone who isn't a management-speaker, especially in the IT department.

soft pedal (verb): to play down or cover up: 'Let's soft pedal on the limitations of that product: when it's **big banged** it'll be **ruggedized**.'

soup to nuts: see **from soup to nuts**.

squaring the circle (phrase): an impossible problem in geometry, used metaphorically to mean a hopeless task. Management-speakers will greatly enjoy being asked to explain this one.

step-change (noun): big change. For example, 'We'll need to see a step-change in our culture before we can implement this policy.'

step up to the plate (phrase): to volunteer: 'We need a **key** manager to step up to the plate and give a presentation on achieving **continuous improvement**.'

> *Work is always so much more fun than fun.*
> **Noel Coward**

stick-to-your-knitting strategy (phrase): policy of sticking to what you're traditionally good at, but with the added bonus of bringing to mind a humorous image of the CEO halfway through a cable-knit cardigan.

strategic fit (noun): how easily a strategy can be put into practice – which might be affected by budget and other resources. For example, 'Do we have strategic fit here, or will we have to **table** it until there's more **skin in the game**?'

stratical (adjective): ridiculous and totally unnecessary combination of strategic and tactical.

streamline (verb): see **downsize**, **rightsize**, **workforce optimization**.

stretch target (noun): a hard-to-reach goal: 'This **upside potential** is achievable if we reach these stretch targets.'

suboptimal (adjective): rubbish.

sunsetting (verb): euphemism for 'closing down': 'Project X is sunsetting: it's become unfeasible.'

swim with the sharks (phrase): to compete for higher stakes but run the risk of having your head bitten off by a Great White. (It's a nice image.)

swing for the fence (phrase): aim high. (Note the baseball terminology.) For example, 'We need to set some **stretch**

targets and really swing for the fence with this new growth strategy.'

sync up (verb): to meet: 'Let's sync up and bounce a few ideas around.'

synergy (noun): management-speakers love this word, which they often use simply as a synonym for 'benefit'. They also use it as a verb ('synergize') and an adjective ('synergistic') and put it into meaningless phrases such as 'contributive synergy'.

table (verb): to postpone. For example, 'Let's table that until Brian's **rolled up** the figures.'

take a bath (phrase): euphemism for losing lots of money.

take a temperature check (phrase): assess. For example, 'Take a temperature check on product sales: we might have to revise our **brand management** strategy.'

take-home message (phrase): message.

take offline (phrase): see **talk offline**.

take one for the team (verb): to take the blame on behalf of the company. Managers usually expect this of their staff rather than doing it themselves.

take ownership (verb): see **own**.

talk offline (phrase): talk outside the current meeting. Management-speakers might also 'take something offline'.

talk track (noun): a memorized sales pitch: 'Make sure the tele-sales people stick to the talk track – we had a complaint over a **bait and switch**.'

tank (verb): to lose money quickly. 'The new product tanked: it was a **learning experience**.'

team player (noun): the number one **competency** for any job.

think outside the box (phrase): think creatively or later-ally. Management will come up with all their brilliant ideas this way.

throw something at the wall and see if it sticks (phrase): see **run something up the flagpole and see if anyone salutes**.

throw the dead cat in someone else's backyard (phrase): dump a problem on somebody else without telling them: 'It was obvious the project was **circling the drain** so we threw the dead cat in Marketing's backyard.' Also **throw something over the wall**.

thrust area (noun): this sounds disturbing, but in fact just means an area of high investment or marketing.

tick all the (right) boxes (phrase): to meet criteria or objectives: 'Our product ticked all the right boxes for the client base, so no one can understand why it **tanked**.'

tin (noun): IT term for hardware. As with words such as **box**, management will use it hoping for the chance to explain it and seem to be technically knowledgeable.

tipping point (noun): see **event horizon**.

to die for (phrase): middle-aged management-speakers will use phrases like this thinking they sound groovy: 'I've got a new product spec that's to die for.'

top line (noun): total revenue: 'What's the top line and does it meet with budget expectations?'

touch base (phrase): management speakers always 'touch base' rather than communicate or meet: 'Here at Acme, we like to touch base with our clients in order to continually improve service.'

townhall meeting (noun): big internal company meeting

where questions are submitted to the panel of executives in writing beforehand – a bit like a press conference for the staff, but without the element of surprise.

treeware (noun): ridiculous way of saying 'paper'.

under the radar (phrase): under surveillance. 'The new **big wheel** in Finance is under the radar since he suggested cutting back on expenses.'

uninstall (verb): to sack.

upsell (verb): to convince a customer to buy extra products or services: 'If the client seems pleased with the **PVM**, try to upsell to the more expensive version.'

upside potential (phrase): the opposite of **downside risk**.

upskill (verb): to **sharpen one's saw.**

up to speed (phrase): fully informed: 'Key managers should all be up to speed on the company's **core** values and mission statement.'

V

value-added (adjective): extra features added on to a product 'free' in order to improve **PVM** and also make it more difficult for customers to compare with competitors' products. Can also be used as a noun to mean 'benefit': 'Is there any value-added in transfering that project to Marketing?'

value-driven (adjective): see **results-driven**.

W

walk the talk (phrase): being able to do what you say you can. You can probably guess the full and excruciating explanation of this phrase.

war story (noun): a (usually long and uninteresting) story told by a salesperson about a particularly difficult sale.

warm and fuzzy (phrase): something cute, friendly or that has the feel-good factor. It can also mean 'acceptable': for example, 'ethical investing is warm and fuzzy capitalism'. An ad campaign might be warm and fuzzy if it uses images of kittens or babies.

water-cooler moment (phrase): gossip. For example, in a meeting you might have a 'water cooler moment' before getting back to the serious business at hand.

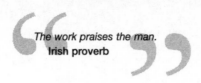

The work praises the man.
Irish proverb

where the rubber meets the road (phrase): salespeople might tell you they're 'out there where the rubber meets the road' or 'on the front line', if they're being particularly irritating.

wins (noun): gains.

win-win (adjective): mutually beneficial: 'We're in a win-win situation on this: we're **empowering** the clients with a much better product which will help them to achieve their goals, while we're gaining higher levels of profit and market share.'

WOMBAT: Waste Of Money, Brains And Time. Another example of management humour.

workforce optimization (noun): see **rightsize**, **down-size**, **streamline**.

work-life balance (phrase): something that the HR department says the company wants to achieve for its staff – but it rarely actually does.

zero-drag (adjective): something without drawbacks. For example, a **clockless worker** is a zero-drag employee.

zero-sum (noun): see **no-brainer**.